The A

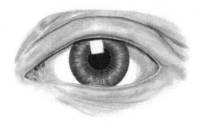

The Answer Is YOU

The Answer Is YOU

A Guide to Mental, Emotional, and Spiritual Freedom

Joseph P. Kauffman

Conscious Collective, LLC
conscious-collective.com

The Answer Is YOU

Joseph P. Kauffman

ISBN-13: 978-0-692-88691-5

ॐ नमः शिवाय

The Answer Is YOU

Dedication

This book is dedicated to YOU. I sincerely hope that this book will help to lead you to the deepest part of yourself, so that you may awaken to who you really are, and be free of the suffering that stems from living a life trying to be who you are not. It is my greatest joy to offer this book to you, and I hope that it will help you realize that you do not have to look for peace, love, and freedom in the world, for these qualities can only be found within the Truth of your own Being.

I would also like to dedicate this book to the amazing people at the Paititi Institute in Peru, for their selfless service, community involvement, and genuine compassion for humanity. Thank you for being such a critical influence on my journey.

.

The Answer Is YOU

Contents

Introduction

There comes a time in most people's lives when they are driven to ask themselves the question: "Who am I?" The questions "What is my purpose?" "What is the meaning of life?" and "Why does the universe exist?" are essentially all different versions of this one fundamental desire to know oneself.

In ancient Kemet, which is known today as Egypt, every temple and lodge that served as a scientific or spiritual learning center had the words "Know Thyself" inscribed above the entrance. It was the fundamental belief of these people that all psychological and emotional suffering arose from one's ignorance of their true nature. We can certainly relate to this belief in our modern culture, as a lack of purpose, guidance, and understanding can often lead to confusion, frustration, and depression, and it is this suffering that often pushes people to begin the search for who they are and how they can be free of their suffering.

It is not only the people of Kemet who realized this inherent cause of suffering, but many other ancient cultures as well. More than two thousand years ago the Buddha also discovered the causes of suffering, and he attributed them to ignorance of one's true nature, as well as the craving and aversion that stems from this ignorance. The Buddha argued that to be free of suffering, we must eliminate these causes of our suffering, and awaken to the Truth of who we are.

The Zen master Yasutani Roshi stated that, *"The fundamental delusion of humanity is to suppose that 'I am here and you are there'."* To the average person this would not seem like a delusion at all, as we feel very deeply that we exist here, within our skins, and that the world and all of the people in it exist outside of us. While this is the common perspective of our culture, it is indeed our fundamental delusion as well, and it is this lack of understanding of the true nature of reality that has given rise to our suffering and has extended to the suffering of other species, and to the planetary organism as a whole.

Because we feel ourselves to be separate from the world in which we live, we have also grown to feel quite alone in this world. Our sense of loneliness and isolation not only makes us feel depressed and miserable, but it also causes us to be anxious and afraid of the world and everyone in it. Because of this inherent fear, we put up all kinds of barriers to protect us from the world—barriers that we have created to keep us safe, but that really end up making us feel more alone, more miserable, and more afraid, as they prevent us from being our natural selves.

Along with the protective barriers that we put up comes a desire to further ensure our protection by glorifying our self-image, in an attempt to fit in and feel accepted by others. We invest far too much time and energy in trying to impress other people, worrying about whether they will judge us or not, and even judging ourselves according to others' standards. We have confused our true identity with our social image, and because we no longer know who we are, we depend on the survival and strength of this image for our own feelings of acceptance and worth.

We have become disconnected from our true selves, and naturally, this has produced a deep sense of lack in our lives, causing us to endlessly search for happiness in objects, experiences, and people to fill the emptiness and make us feel whole again. We crave pleasure, material riches, and stimulating experiences—anything that will distract us from this inherent lack of connection. But no matter how hard we try to escape it, eventually the sensation returns. And that is because we are looking for the answer to our freedom in all the wrong places. We are looking for freedom in the world, when the answer to ending our suffering lies within us. Until we heal the root cause of our suffering, and awaken to our true nature, our inherent confusion will continue to manifest itself in the world around us.

It is because we feel that we are separate from nature that we also feel it is okay to manipulate it, pollute it, and cause it harm. We project our inner turmoil onto the planet, causing outer turmoil. Nearly all of the disasters of our time—war, famine, oppression, social injustice, environmental pollution, extinction—arise from this delusional belief that we have an existence independent of the world we live in. All of this misery, all of this destruction, all of this pain and suffering, is caused by our failure to realize that there is no separation and that really we are all one.

Just as the suffering of an individual pushes them to know more about their true nature, the suffering of society pushes us to question our collective nature and what it is that we are really doing as a species. The state of the world now is calling us to make a choice: evolution or extinction. Clearly we cannot continue to operate at our current level of consciousness, and so, this is a wonderful opportunity for us as a species to evolve past our ignorant and self-destructive beliefs and create a better society, one that understands our connection to each other and the planet, and one that is focused on love and unity, rather than fear and separation.

But society is made of individuals, and this decision to evolve must happen on the individual level, and not a single being can be excluded. We cannot heal the world unless we heal ourselves. By healing our ignorant beliefs and finding peace within ourselves, together we can create peace on earth—but only if we make the choice individually. We cannot continue to live ignorantly and wait for someone else to save us; we must take responsibility for our own behavior and how we are impacting the world.

The way we perceive the world determines how we interact with it, and our perception always follows our beliefs and the opinions that we have agreed upon. Therefore, in order to change our behavior we must first change our worldviews and our belief systems. If we are to have any hope of ending the destruction we are doing to the planet and to ourselves, there must be a radical shift in our perception and the way that we think and relate to the world.

Just as a baby takes its first steps, as a child has his first ride on a bicycle without training wheels, or as a teenager takes his first unaccompanied drive in a car, once we expand our limits life has changed and will never be the same. By taking this next step in our evolution, and healing this belief of separation, we can expand our limits, and change our lives for the better. With this change in perception comes a love, a peace, and a freedom that words are incapable of describing, and many people who have already made this leap can attest to this.

The fact of our oneness is not only something that I have realized in my own experience, it is an ancient truth held by many philosophies such as those of the Hindu philosophy of Advaita Vedanta, by Taoism, by many branches of Buddhism, including Zen, by Islamic Sufism, as well as by some branches of Christianity that follow the Gospel of Thomas and the Essene Gospel of Peace.

Modern science is finally confirming what these ancient wisdom traditions have known for centuries, and I intend to share this knowledge with you and help you understand it so that you may finally allow yourself to be free, but I will need you to meet me halfway. In the words of the famous Zen saying, "*I can open the door, but you must walk through it.*"

Just as you cannot accurately convey the taste of an orange to someone who has never had one, words cannot accurately convey the Truth. You can only realize the Truth within yourself, through your own direct experience. The words in this book are only words, but they point to something much greater. It is up to you whether you want to get caught in the words, or see the greater reality that they are pointing to.

This reality is nothing to fear; it is the reality of who you are, it is the knowledge that will give you peace, the wisdom that will give you understanding, and the Truth that will free you from the prison of delusional, negative, and conditioned thinking. There is no need for you to suffer the way that you do, to stress over life's challenges, to fear life's uncertainties, or to cling to life's comforts.

You can be free of this suffering, and with this book I intend to show you that the answer to ending your suffering, as well as the suffering of society and of innumerable other beings, will not be found in the world, for the answer is YOU. Only you can free yourself by acknowledging your own conditioning, transcending your limited beliefs, and awakening to your true identity. Allow the knowledge in this book to help you awaken from the illusion of separation, to free you from your suffering, to point you to the dimension of peace and oneness within yourself, and to help you realize the Truth of who you really are.

"A human being is a part of the whole called by us universe, a part limited in time and space. He experiences himself, his thoughts and feelings as something separated from the rest, a kind of optical delusion of his consciousness. This delusion is a kind of prison for us, restricting us to our personal desires and to affection for a few persons nearest to us. Our task must be to free ourselves from this prison by widening our circle of compassion to embrace all living creatures and the whole of nature in its beauty."

—*Albert Einstein*

The Answer Is YOU

1   Truth

I have been talking a lot about the Truth, and I have mentioned the importance of realizing the Truth if we want to find peace and be free of our suffering, but what exactly is the Truth? In the spiritual traditions of the East, there is a philosophy known as "The Two Truths." This philosophy can be very helpful to us when it comes to understanding exactly what is that we mean when we speak of "the Truth."

The Two Truths are *relative* truth and *absolute* Truth. Relative truth is that which is true in relation to one's perception or circumstances. For example, it would be true if someone in Peru were to say that the United States is located in the North. But for someone in Canada, it would also be true to say that the United States is located in the South. Both people would be speaking the truth, but this truth is *relative* to their particular circumstances.

Many things that we believe to be the absolute Truth are actually only relative truths. Most people would agree when looking at a blade of grass that the color of grass is green. But this is only true in relation to someone who can perceive color. It would not be true to someone who is colorblind. Not to mention that when we say something is "green" it is only because we have agreed to call it by that name. There is no way to be absolutely sure that we are seeing the exact same color, that your green is my green, as we can only see the color green from our unique perspective.

We might also agree that the internal temperature of a volcano is very hot, but again, this is only true in relation to the senses of the human body. This would not be true in relation to the sun, which is estimated to be over twenty five million degrees Fahrenheit. Much of what we consider to be the absolute Truth—light, dark, hot, cold, big, small, good, bad, etc.—are only relative truths.

The absolute Truth is not so easy to discover, and it is the absolute Truth of existence that we are concerned with knowing here. When we want to know the absolute Truth of something, we do not want to be fooled by our perceptions or by changing circumstances. Knowing Truth cannot mean to know one thing, only for it to become something else later depending on conditions.

If a friend told you they were in India, only to tell you the next day that it was Japan, how can that be the Truth? Truth requires consistency. Truth is that which is beyond change, and thus is never changing. To discover this never-changing and absolute Truth of life, you will have to look beyond the aspects of your experience that are constantly changing. To do this often requires looking at your experience in a completely new and unfamiliar way.

2 The Parable of the Empty Cup

There was once a young martial artist who was seeking a master to train with. As the master would explain facets of his training and philosophy, the student would frequently interrupt by saying, *"Oh yes, I know that."* One day, the master began pouring the student a cup of tea, and kept pouring until the cup generously overflowed. The student jumped up before the tea scalded him and demanded to know, *"How can such a great master spill tea like that?"* The master stopped pouring and replied, *"If you wish to sample my tea, you must first empty your cup."*

This old parable points out that if we want to discover something new, we must first empty our minds of the notion that we already understand what it is we are seeking. This seems obvious enough, but many of us cling to what we think we know, and we allow our preconceived notions to interfere and prevent us from gaining any new knowledge. We often try to force the experience we want to have, instead of allowing the experience we were meant to have, and in doing this, we miss out on gaining any new insight or understanding.

We must learn to let go of our expectations and preconceived notions, and allow ourselves to just experience reality openly. The usefulness of a cup lies in its emptiness. When one wants to drink a cup of tea, they do not seek a cup that is already full. So too, if we want to fill our minds with new knowledge we must first empty our minds of the opinions and beliefs that fill it. The greatest tea in the world cannot be tasted from a cup that is already full.

An empty mind is a prerequisite for Truth. We cannot learn if we are stuck in our mind's conditioned way of thinking. We must be open to discovering the Truth, whatever it may turn out to be. This requires a state of openness, curiosity, and sincerity, a state of pure awareness, a state of observing reality without jumping to conclusions about what reality is.

This state of direct experience is known in Zen as "beginner's mind," and it is essential to embody this state when we want to understand our experience. According to the Zen tradition, they believe that every moment we should embody this state of beginner's mind, for every moment is new, and to compare the new and unknown to what we have learned in the past only limits us from understanding the present moment that we are now experiencing.

We must be able to reform ourselves into blank canvases many times in our lives, and in doing so we can gain a new sense of clarity, new insights, and new knowledge. This is important to keep in mind when we are setting out on the uncharted waters of the unknown. We must not look for what we think we might find, but be open and accepting of whatever it is that presents itself to us.

The Answer Is YOU

3 Perception

At this moment, you are experiencing these words and reading this book. You can see this book with your eyes; you can touch it with the skin of your hand and feel its texture; maybe you can even smell it if you bring your nose close enough. Rubbing your fingers along the page may produce some sound that you can hear with your ears, and if you wanted to, licking it may produce some taste on your tongue. Is not your experience of this book solely based on your five sense organs: eyes, nose, skin, ears, and tongue? As you experience other objects in the world outside of you, can you conclude that this is true for all of them? Or is there another way to experience the world?

In order to understand the absolute Truth of our life experience, we should look deeply into these sense organs with which our experience so exclusively happens. These sense organs allow us to perceive information from the environment around us, and without them we could not have any sensory experience.

While our sense organs allow us to perceive a vast array of information, we are still limited in the ways in which we are able to experience the world. Dolphins, bats, and other animals are able to use echolocation as a means of perceiving their environment—an ability far beyond our human capabilities. Bumblebees use the hair on their legs to detect a flower's electromagnetic field, and sharks can perceive differences between the electrical charge of an animal and the water around it. These are just few of many examples showing clearly that humans are quite limited in the amount of senses with which we can perceive our environment.

Not only are we limited in the quantity of our senses, but also in the quality of our senses. A dog would be able to smell this book from quite far away, a snake would be able to see the temperature of the book because of its advanced heat-sensing vision, and an X-ray machine could make an image of the inside of the book. We do not need to look any deeper to understand that what we experience through our senses is only a fraction of whatever really exists "out there."

Our experience of reality is not only limited by our five senses, but by many other things as well. For example, consider the influence that your emotions have on your experience. Our shifting attitudes create numerous biochemicals in the body, and these chemicals alter our sensory perception and change the lens through which we experience. How different would your experience of this book be if you were angry? What about if you were ecstatic with joy, depressed, or thinking about someone you love?

How do your desires influence your experience of this book? Do you think this book would be experienced differently if you had no interest in what was being said? What about if you felt you needed this book for the information it contains or purely as a source of entertainment, would your perception of it then be different? What if you were extremely hungry or tired at the moment, how might your perception of this book be altered? Can you see how your focus plays a major role in what you experience each moment?

How much of your experience of this book depends, too, on the books that you have experienced in the past? If you think that this book is short or long, would that not depend on the length of the books that you have previously read? If you happened to come from a culture that had never seen a book at all, how different would your perception of this book be? Do you think you would already know its function, or would you perhaps find a new function for the book, one that would be unfamiliar to someone who has read a book before?

When you move a little to the side or tilt your head, how does it change your perception of the book? What about after exposing it to a bright light, or placing it against a wall, does your perception of it change? Would hitting the book with a pen produce a different sound than tapping it with your finger? Would you perceive this book differently if it were dirty or smelled bad? What does it mean that your experience of this book changes so radically depending on how you use your senses, on the interaction between your senses, and on changes in your environment?

If you were to move away from this book and close your eyes, what would happen to the book? Would it still be there? How can you be *absolutely* sure it is not some mystical book that pops into existence the moment you look at it? If its very existence is so questionable the moment you turn off your sensory perception, how accountable are your senses for its existence? Without sensory perception of this book, is its existence even worth considering?

Whatever we experience in the world outside of us is highly colored by the vast amount of things occurring within us—our senses, our emotions, our desires, our focus, our intention, our past experiences, and past naming of things—all of these create a filter for our perception, determining how we experience reality.

What can you say or think about this book that can be considered the *absolute* Truth? And is this question not applicable for every other thing that you perceive in the world around you? Thus, when trying to find the Truth about ourselves and our experience, the experience itself is simply unable to provide it. Would the answer then lie in the "**you**" that is experiencing?

4 YOU

Who are you—the real you—deep down in the core of your being? Who is the you that remains beyond all appearances and changing circumstances? What is the absolute Truth of your existence?

If you are like most people, it is likely that you have no clue who you really are, and this is perfectly okay, for it is only once you admit that you do not know who you are that you are then capable of seeing through all that you are not and discovering your True Self. Being raised in this society, you have been conditioned to mistakenly identify yourself with your name, your body, your self-image, your personal history, your profession, your likes and dislikes, your culture, and the many roles you play in your life—but none of these things are really you.

In Sanskrit there is a phrase called, "*neti, neti*" which translates as "no, no" or "not this, not this." The meaning of this phrase refers to a process in which we look at our lives and look at ourselves, inquiring into the many things we believe ourselves to be, and in doing so, we shed away the layers of what we are not, being left only with our True

Selves in the end. It is similar to the process in which a sculptor chisels away at a block of stone to reveal the object hidden within it. By removing the layers of false identification, one by one, we can reveal the True nature of our being which lies hidden within us.

When someone asks us who we are, we usually reply by stating our name; but you are not your name—your existence cannot be confined to a label that was given to you at birth. Nor can you be the image of yourself that you have attached to your name. Almost everyone has some image of themselves—some idea of who they think they are. But this image is made entirely of thoughts; it has no basis in reality. It consists of the many things that we have falsely identified with—our personal history being one of them.

Many people allow what has happened to them in their past to become a part of their identity, and often they suffer greatly because of this. No matter what may or may not have happened to you in the past, the past is gone, it exists only in your memory. If you suffer from something that happened in the past it is because you have yet to forgive the situation and move on. But it should be obvious that your past is not who you are. Didn't you exist before anything happened to you in your past? So how can your past be you?

Are you your beliefs then? Can you fully identify yourself with some religion, belief system, or philosophy? Can you define yourself as a Christian, a Buddhist, a Muslim, a Jew, an Atheist, a democrat, a republican? While these belief systems may provide certain values, they are not who you are. You cannot be confined to a perspective that you adopted after birth. Who were you before you adopted your beliefs, before you were taught to view the world as you now see it?

Are you your personality? Carl Jung, one of the greatest psychologists of our time, described the personality as the continual sum of all of the people we have ever met, and all of the experiences we have ever had. Your personality is not a static thing; it is fluid and constantly changing, being shaped by the circumstances of your experience. The personality is what forms our distinctive character; it is the individual differences that we have in patterns of thinking, feeling, and behavior. We all have a unique personality because we each experience reality in a way that is unique to us, but the personality is not who we are at our core.

It is interesting to note that the word personality comes from the Latin word "*persona*" which refers to a social role or character played by an actor. And just as we are not our individual personalities, we are not the social roles that we play either. Many people identify with their roles—they believe themselves to be their profession, their occupation in society, or their position in the family. We play many roles in life, and just like all of our experiences, our roles are constantly changing. We play the role of mother or father, daughter or son, sister or brother, student or teacher, employee or supervisor, man or woman. Our roles shift along with our changing circumstances, but we are not our roles.

And what good is any role without an actor—without somebody playing the role? But who is the one that is playing the many roles in your life? Is it your body? In our culture, we are taught from a very young age to identify with our bodies, and as we develop, we believe these bodies to be who we really are—but is this the Truth? You can only experience your body through your highly limited senses, which themselves are a part of your body. Just as for this book, your experience of your body is exceptionally narrow. The real you cannot be described as young or old, black or white, fat or slim, attractive or ugly, because those are all relative terms that depend on your senses, moods, past experiences, and so forth.

And isn't your body always changing? This body that you have now is not the same body that you had at birth. Every cell of your body is constantly dying and being reborn, so how can it be the *you* that remains beyond all appearances and changing circumstances?

What about the constitution of your body—what is it made of? Is not every cell in your body derived from your environment, fueled by the water, food, air, and energy that you consume? Was not every atom of your body formed in the core of exploding stars, billions of years ago? Is not your body just as connected to the Universe as a tree is to the earth? And what if someone were to accidently cut off your leg, or some part of your body, would that make *you* any more or less you? Is not your body something that is separate from you, something that exists apart from *you*?

YOU

Look deeply into all that you think yourself to be today—is it not all based on past experiences, on what you have learned or adopted from your culture? Whatever you experienced through your limited senses was but a fraction of what may have truly happened, and how well do you remember these fractional experiences that form your identity? How can a fractional memory of a lifetime of fractional experiences tell you the Truth about who you are?

After inquiring into the nature of your existence, you may come to the conclusion that, in essence, you are not your body, nor your name, nor your personality, nor your history, nor the roles that you play in life. Perhaps, then, the answer to who you are lies in your thoughts and feelings— but are they not also always changing, appearing, and disappearing? Can you observe your thoughts, and if so, how can they be you? Is not whatever you can observe something outside of you, something that cannot be you, whether it is a book, your body, your personality, your past, your thoughts or your feelings?

Whenever you observe something, what you observe is a thing, an object. This implies that there is someone observing: call it the observer, the witness, or the subject. Do you not think of "your thoughts," and "your feelings," as in "your phone" and "your house"? Does that not make your thoughts and feelings into things that are separate from you, things that are not you?

Have you ever tried simply sitting and observing your thoughts? If not, give yourself a moment to try it now. Just sit, close your eyes, and observe whatever arises in the field of your conscious awareness. When thoughts come, don't try to make sense of them or fuel them with more thoughts, just witness them, and allow them to come and go as they please. With a little time, you will begin to feel the presence that precedes the thoughts, and you will recognize that you are not your thoughts, but the witness of the thoughts.

If you participated in this small experiment, or have any experience with meditation, you will also realize that it is quite difficult to remain in this state of pure observation without being distracted by thought. But if you are capable of sustaining a longer period of time simply observing without thinking, then you must also be well aware that when your thoughts are gone, you are still there. Even if you cannot stop your thoughts on command, moments come when naturally you are not thinking anything, and during these moments are you not still there?

Are you now becoming more aware of the essence that lies beyond thought, the awareness in which thought exists—your witnessing consciousness? Is this the Truth of who you are—the *you* that lies beyond all appearances and circumstances? Is the one *you* that you are the awareness that cannot be directly experienced, yet is always experiencing? Have you now discovered your true nature by removing that which cannot really be you?

5 The True YOU

Throughout your life this witnessing consciousness has been present. It is you, but you cannot say much more about it, other than saying what it is not—which is why mystics tend to speak of it in negative terms such as *neti, neti,* or *not this, not this.* It is *not* your body, *not* your mind, *not* your personality, *not* your thoughts or feelings, or any of the things that you have mistakenly identified with. It is your witnessing presence, your fundamental awareness, the very essence of your being. You can find nothing to be other than that—at least not in any permanent or absolute way. It is the one quality of your being that you can be sure of, the one Truth that you can never escape. You simply are, always, witnessing.

In the Hindu tradition, your witnessing consciousness is referred to as the Self. However, this is just a name, and no name can truly describe the pure essence of consciousness that is YOU. But you can still feel this essence that is you, even if you cannot accurately define it. Simply by trying to define or label ourselves we limit ourselves to that label, and a label is not who we are. No label can define the immensity of your True nature. You are the awareness that precedes every label, the awareness that is perceiving these words and turning them into thoughts, the awareness that creates the world with every act of observation.

You cannot be aware of yourself, for you are awareness itself. How can a witness *witness* itself? That is like trying to see your own eyes without a reflection, or cut a knife with the tip of its own blade—it is impossible. The subject can only observe the object; it cannot make an object out of itself. But by the very act of observing, you indirectly know yourself as the observer, as the subject. No witnessing of the witness is needed to prove its existence.

This is the dilemma that modern science has when it tries to come up with a definition for consciousness. The modern scientist attempts to step outside of himself in order to observe himself, an attempt that is always doomed to failure. You cannot make an object out of your subjective experience, but you know that consciousness exists, simply because you exist.

Being, in itself, is proof of your existence, so it is also quite clear that you are not nothing, otherwise who would be there to know that they are nothing? Only one who exists can say "I don't exist." To be aware of the world, of nothingness, or of anything at all, you first have to *be*. This essential state of being is who you are, only you have forgotten who you are because you have been led away from your source. You have lost touch with your true nature by being raised and conditioned in a society in which everyone else is also out of touch with their true nature.

Think about why it is so difficult to know who you really are. If you could be your name, your body, or your position in society, then the question would be easy to answer. If you were something that had a form, with a certain characteristic or quality, then you would actually be that form and there would be no uncertainty about it. But consciousness is something that exists outside of space, outside of time, and thus is without form. This is the reason why your observing consciousness often goes unnoticed, even though it is always there, and you are always it. It is no *thing*—no object with form, but just simply, undeniably, *you*.

This witnessing consciousness, this formless dimension of yourself, is the awareness in which your experience happens, yet it remains untouched by this experience at all times. It is similar to the background of white on which you are reading these words. This white background allows any and every word to exist within it, yet it is not confined to any of these words. Similarly, your awareness allows any and every form to exist within it, but it is not bound to any of these forms.

Existing without form or quality, this consciousness also has no miserable or joyful past, no dreams or doubts about the future, no beliefs to fight over or defend, no pain or struggle to tolerate, no body to criticize or improve. When you reconnect with yourself as pure awareness, all of those just fade away, revealing themselves as things that are separate from you.

We only suffer when we falsely identify with the objects that arise in our awareness, rather than with the awareness itself—when we identify with our thoughts, with our emotions, our personal history, and the many stories we tell ourselves. When you reconnect to your source—the essence of your being, the pure and impartial witness—you become free from all of the troubles of the material world; free from the world of form. You no longer feel the desire to cling to forms or depend on them for your happiness. Instead, you are free to enjoy form, free to let form be, and free to allow all forms to come and go as they please. All forms are impermanent and changing, but your consciousness, being formless, is eternal, and exists regardless of the forms that it gives life to.

Without form or quality what could change? How can something that has no form ever die? It can't because it was never born. It simply is. It is existence itself. In Sanskrit, this subjective experience of the ultimate, unchanging reality is described as *Satchitananda* or Truth (*Sat*), Consciousness (*Chit*), Bliss (*Ananda*). Your true being, as Consciousness, is ever at peace, ever at rest, eternally existing in the dimension of here and now. It is the formless and eternal quality within you that expresses itself through the world of form.

Since all forms are undergoing constant change, shouldn't it be obvious that the absolute and unchanging Truth of who you are must be without form? Could you imagine accomplishing anything, saying anything, or thinking anything without this formless consciousness being present? It is impossible to imagine, because how could any of the things that you do happen without someone inside of you—that is you—experiencing what is happening? Who would be there to adjust to circumstances, adapt to the environment, develop, and grow? Without consciousness, nothing can happen and nothing can be experienced. You can do things without acknowledging it or thinking about it, but it is still always present. You cannot even be unaware of it without it being there. You, as Consciousness, are essential to everything, the essence of everything, and without your witnessing, there is no reality that can be witnessed.

"At the center of the Universe dwells the Great Spirit; and that center is really everywhere.
It is within each of us."

– Black Elk

The Answer Is YOU

6 The Cosmic YOU

As we discovered earlier, your sensory experience of this book and the rest of the Universe did not allow you to know with absolute certainty whether or not it actually exists. Suppose that the Universe outside of you really doesn't exist; then the only thing that truly exists without changing is YOU, Consciousness. Or suppose that, irrespective of your limited and influenced perceptions of it, the Universe outside of you really does exist, independent of your personal experience. How could the other people within the Universe function without such a similar consciousness inside them? How could they experience anything, think anything, do anything, say anything? In yourself, it is easily recognizable that your awareness is essential to any experience. Why would it be any different for someone else? And how could animals, plants, cells, or any being exist without such a witnessing entity? They cannot, just as you cannot.

If your consciousness is without form, without quality, and without characteristics of any kind, would that not imply that the consciousness in every other being is also formless? And if they are all without form, how can you distinguish their consciousness from your own? What forms would you use to compare them? Isn't the observing you exactly the same as the observing them?

It is easy to compare and contrast things with form, but how do you compare two things that are without form, that have no qualities to set them apart? In what way could you define your awareness as being any different from the awareness in someone else? Are you not identical to them?

The consciousness inhabiting your body is exactly the same as the consciousness inhabiting my body. We are one. The delusion that we are separate beings comes from identifying with the world of form—with our names, our bodies, our roles, our beliefs, our thoughts, and all of the mental constructs that we have created; but even these are more connected to the universe than we realize.

Your body and my body are both totally made up of and dependent upon the elements of the earth—the water, the air, the heat, the land, the soil and the food it produces—as well as all of the elements that these elements are dependent upon—the sun, the stars, the galaxies, and a vast field of energy and space to contain them in. Nature is our extended body, and the elements outside of our skin are just as important to our health as the elements within our skin. Our bodies are connected to the universe as a whole, and consequently to each other and the many ways in which we influence our shared environment.

The Cosmic YOU

When we look at a tree, we do not see the tree for what it really is. We see how it appears to us on the surface, and we dismiss it as being just another form in the Universe. We fail to realize that the tree is connected to the Universe on every level; that all of nature is expressing itself through that single form. There can be no tree without the earth that it grows from, the sun that gives it energy, the water that nourishes its growth, and the millions of fungi and bacteria fertilizing its soil. Looking deeply into anything in nature, we realize that it is connected to the whole. We see that nature is one seamless web, and the notion that things have an existence of their own is merely an illusion.

This is the meaning behind the famous astronomer Carl Sagan's quote: *"If you wish to make an apple pie from scratch, you must first invent the Universe."* All forms only exist in relation to all other forms. This is as true for a tree or an apple pie as it is for your body and mind. You do not have an existence independent of your environment, but rather you are your environment, and your environment is you. You are just as connected to the Universe as a finger is to a hand, or as a branch is to a tree. The entire cosmos is expressing itself through your being.

In Buddhism, this phenomenon of our inter-connectedness is referred to as *"Shunyata"* or "Emptiness." Buddhist philosophy points out that the true nature of all forms is essentially formless. Forms do not have an existence of their own, but rather they arise together, and are mutually dependent on one another. Everything in the world of form is constantly changing, constantly dying, and constantly being reborn—which is why Buddhists say that there is no-self; no form that has an existence in and of itself.

According to Zen Buddhists, all things have their existence in The Void. The Void is that which is no-thing, but contains all things within it, or as some Christian mystics state, *"God is Nothing; He is Utterly Other; He is the VOID."*

We fail to see the oneness of all things, and because of this, we unknowingly cause a lot of harm to ourselves. We pollute the Earth that we live on, cut down the trees that produce our oxygen, destroy the ecosystems of nature and the animals that maintain them, and we mistreat and harm each other, thinking that these destructive actions will not have a direct effect on us. All of this suffering arises from failing to see the interconnectedness of all forms, as well as failing to see the formless dimension of consciousness that we all share.

Just think what would happen if you were to add two entirely formless and identical Consciousnesses; would you end up with two—or would they simply combine into one? Being formless, would they even need to combine in order to become one? Are they not just one formless Consciousness wherever they are? And since every being has such an absolutely identical Consciousness within them, does this not mean that the Universe has only one Consciousness, looking through many eyes, hearing through numerous ears, and tasting through countless tongues? Are not the many, in Truth, just one?

Every being experiences themselves as the center of their experience. Consciousness is what lies at our very core, and connects us all to each other. We may appear to be separate and individual because of the various forms our Consciousness inhabits, but below the surface the substance of our being is one and the same.

"A thousand heads hath Purusha (Consciousness), a thousand eyes, a thousand feet.

On every side pervading the earth he fills a space ten fingers wide."

– Rig Veda

We are so fascinated by the complexity and beauty of the various forms in nature, that we have been led away from the formless dimension of Consciousness that lies at our very center. When you look at a person, you see many differences in their unique form, and often we compare, contrast, and judge one another because of the forms that we inhabit. But if you look beyond the various qualities and characteristics of form, and look another person in the eyes, you see a Being, and it is this Being that lies beneath the surface of form that connects us all. That is why the eyes are often referred to as the gateway to the soul, because they allow us to see and feel the presence of another Being, and realize our oneness.

The Answer Is YOU

We are like waves in the ocean, each with a unique character and quality on the surface, but deep down we are eternally connected to one another and to the ocean as a whole. If you practice looking beyond the surface of appearances, you will begin to see the true Being that lies within each form. You will see your Consciousness looking through the eyes of another, and it is when you see yourself in another that you cannot help but develop compassion for them; because in Truth, there is no "them," there is only YOU, experiencing yourself from an inconceivable amount of perspectives.

We are only able to disrespect, mistreat, and harm one another when we forget that the other person is us; when we only see the objects of form, and not the subjective Consciousness that lies within. Lust, greed, violence, selfishness—all arise from perceiving others in terms of their individual differences, seeing them only as bodies, and what we can get from them as bodies, rather than acknowledging the Being that lies within the body.

When we see one another as different aspects of ourselves—as ourselves experiencing a different situation and circumstance—we develop a love, a connection, and a unity that allows us to see beyond the various forms, as well as the various ways that someone may act out when they have forgotten their connection and their formless nature. If you look at another in this light, you will see a Being that is just like you, looking back at you. Just as Ram Dass stated, *"It is like two mirrors facing each other. You see yourself looking at yourself looking at yourself. There is only one of us."* It is the recognition of this oneness and connection with another that gives rise to what we call Love.

The Cosmic YOU

True Love is when you are able to see yourself in another, when you recognize that there is no separation between you and any other Being in the Universe. Only forms can differ, and even then, all forms are dependent upon one another. In Truth, you are limitless, infinite, formless, and eternally connected to the Universe as a whole. Separation is an illusion.

So whether the Universe outside of you really does exist or not, all that we know to truly exist as being fixed, unchanging, and eternal, is YOU, the Universal Consciousness that is present in each and every thing. YOU are the Truth of existence. YOU are the Consciousness that creates form and brings it to life. Without YOU there is no Universe.

You are not limited to this body, to this mind, or to this reality—you are a limitless ocean of Consciousness, imbued with infinite potential. You are existence itself. In the Vedic traditions you are called Brahman, Atman, Vishnu, Purusha, or Shiva.

Jehovah, the Christian name for God derived from the Hebrew Yahweh, (from the letters YHWH), is translated as "I AM." YOU ARE the essence of life—the Cosmic Consciousness that creates, lives in, and destroys all things. In Buddhism, your true nature is referred to as your "Buddha Nature." Muslims refer to it as Allah, Native tribes have often called it the Great Spirit, Taoists refer to it as the Tao, and numerous other cultures throughout history have all created their own distinctive names for it. But the one eternal reality that these cultures point to remains the same—and this reality is YOU.

Think of how this Universe is experienced and defined through your senses. So it is YOU—within this form and in countless other forms throughout the Cosmos in which you are the witness also—the one who observes, experiences, and expresses itself in the world of form. There is nothing or no one else that can define it. As you cannot exist or do anything without your observing Consciousness, how could the universe exist or change without this Cosmic YOU?

How could anything appear and disappear without YOU? Does this not mean that your universal witnessing causes universal creation? If you as Consciousness in each and everything were to stop functioning, how could the Universe continue? Does not everything exist in YOU, rather than you existing in everything? Is not this entire Universe created by the Universal Consciousness, which is thus also called the Creator, or—if you prefer the name—God?

"Has it ever occurred to you that you are seeking God with his eyes?

– Adyashanti

---

7 The Mysterious World of Quantum Physics

For most people, this idea that their true nature is Consciousness, and that they are connected to the Universe as a whole, is quite foreign. Most people perceive themselves to be insignificant creatures in an unintelligent and dispassionate Universe. This belief stems from the worldview that was adopted by Newtonian physics, which views the entire Universe as a random and mechanical process that somehow gave rise to intelligent life.

This is the common belief of our culture, and anything that challenges this belief is often met with much ridicule and resistance. However, new discoveries in quantum physics have completely reshaped our view of reality, and are now confirming what the ancient wisdom traditions have known for centuries.

You are not a small and unimportant creature confined to the form of this physical body, contrary to popular belief. At the core of your being you are pure awareness, and this awareness is the same source from which everything in the Universe arises, exists as, and returns to. Consciousness is the dimension of yourself that you have forgotten you are, and of which you long to return to. Or as Mooji says, *"the place that you are looking for is the place from which you are looking."*

When we are out of touch with our source we feel anxious, lost, and confused. When we are connected to our source we feel peaceful, loving, and relaxed. You do not need to prove your true nature through science in order to trust it and know that it exists. Still, explaining it logically and scientifically can help to ease our analytical minds, and reshape the beliefs that we have adopted from our culture, which views science as an authority figure of truth.

Looking at our hands, we are able to see the size, the shape, and the features on our skin, but we are unable to see what lies beneath this relative view that our vision provides. We cannot directly perceive the many bones, tissues, cells, molecules, and atoms that make up our hands, but without them, our hands could not exist.

Many branches of science are dedicated to studying these microscopic realities, but quantum physics is concerned with the scale of reality that is the most microscopic—the atomic and subatomic scale. Quantum physicists study the very fabric of the Universe, with the notion that by understanding the way reality functions at its core, we can have a greater understanding of how the Universe functions at larger scales, and even how it functions as a whole.[1]

---

[1] Keep in mind that I am not a quantum physicist. I have written my understanding of the research I have done, used only to display that

The Mysterious World of Quantum Physics

By studying nature at the quantum level, physicists have come to some amazing discoveries. Of these discoveries, one that I find to be among the most fascinating is that atoms, what we consider to be the building blocks of all matter, are actually made up of more than 99.999999999999% empty space. To try to illustrate just how vast that is: if the nucleus of an atom were a basketball, then the electrons orbiting the nucleus would be over twenty miles away!

Everything we perceive to be solid and static is made up of almost entirely empty space. What we feel when we touch matter is not the object of matter itself, but the electrostatic field around the atoms of the object repelling against the electrostatic field around the atoms of our skin. This means that we are not actually able to touch anything, for whatever we are feeling is actually the interaction of electrostatic fields, similar to the pressure that is felt when we put together the opposite ends of two magnets.

What is perhaps even more interesting is the fact that this "empty space" is not really empty at all, but is abundant with energy. The empty space within a single hydrogen atom, which is about 10^{-23} cubic centimeters, contains

---

Consciousness is the ultimate reality, not matter. If you would like to better understand quantum physics, I strongly recommend doing your own research. Researching the work of physicists David Bohm, Amit Goswami, Fred Alan Wolf, Thomas Campbell, Nick Herbert, and John Hagelin is a great place to start. It is also worth mentioning that there are different interpretations to the theories I am presenting, and not all quantum physicists agree with each other as to what exactly these experiments mean.

within it a trillion times more energy than all of the mass, of all of the planets, all of the stars, and all of the galaxies, of up to twenty billion light years.

Another fascinating discovery of quantum physics is that all matter is essentially just vibrational energy, oscillating at different frequencies. This means that even rocks, which we perceive to be lifeless, static, and solid, are really living, dancing, and vibrating, at the molecular level. There is nothing in nature that is truly solid; everything is just energy in a state of constant vibration, and the lower its rate of vibration, the denser the matter appears to be.

Time is what gives things the illusion of solidity, but beyond appearances, everything is constantly moving, constantly being born, dying, and being reborn at every moment, including your body as you read these words, as well as the book on which these words are written. Indeed the study of nature at the quantum scale has drastically changed the way we understand the Universe in which we are living.

One of the most famous and repeated experiments in quantum physics is known as The Double-Slit Experiment. In this experiment, physicists set up a screen with two vertical slits cut in it. Behind this screen, they set up a photographic plate. Electrons—little particles of matter—are then shot through the screen with two slits, hitting the photographic plate behind the screen.

If electrons are indeed particles then they should leave a pattern on the photographic plate that is in line with the two slits. Just as if you were to shoot a paintball gun through two slits, you would expect to have two lines of paint on the wall behind it.

But this is not what happens. Instead, an interference pattern is made on the photographic plate, which indicates that the electrons behave as waves. An interference pattern occurs when two waves interfere with each other, similar to if you were to drop two pebbles in a pond side by side. If the crest (top) of one wave meets with the crest of another, it is known as constructive interference. If the crest of a wave meets with the trough (bottom) of another, it is known as destructive interference. When both constructive and destructive interference occur together, it creates an interference pattern such as the one that appears on the photographic plate.

When physicists first discovered that the electrons were behaving as waves, they were left with more questions than answers. How can solid particles of matter create an interference pattern like waves? It would be as surprising as if the paintballs we shot through the two slits didn't make a pattern of two lines, but instead made a wave-like pattern along the wall behind it. Physicists thought that perhaps the particles were somehow bouncing off of each other and creating a pattern that resembled the interference pattern of waves. So, they decided to shoot the electrons through the slits one at a time. Still, the electrons eventually produced an interference pattern on the photographic plate.

In an attempt to figure out what was going on, scientists decided to put electron detectors at the slits to measure which of the slits the electrons were going through. These detectors allowed the physicists to record the data of the experiment so that they could review the data once the experiment was finished.

When they did that, the electrons once again acted like particles, creating a pattern on the photographic plate that was in line with the two slits. It was suspected that the detectors might have been interfering with the experiment. So, they tried turning the detectors on but without recording the data that the detectors were receiving about the electrons. The result was, that the electrons acted like waves again.

It appeared that the very act of recording the data—of measuring, or observing the electrons—determined whether they behaved as particles or waves. In physics this is known as the measurement problem. The measurement problem points out that the nature of an electron changes when you look at it or try to measure it. It collapses from being a wave into a particle in space and time, which is what we see as reality.

This experiment reveals that particles are not really what they appear to be. Particles are momentary manifestations of a deeper level of reality, a reality that physicist David Bohm has named "The Implicate Order." Everything in the universe exists in waveform—exists in the realm of this "Implicate Order"—and only become particles in space and time—only come out of the Implicate Order—once they are observed.

This means that an electron—the core element of what we call our physical reality—is only a solid particle—is only matter—when someone is looking at it. Otherwise, it is a wave, and is not solid at all.

Physicists have always thought of atoms as being dense particles, similar to little marbles. We now know that they are not actually like little marbles, but are really made up of almost entirely empty space, with a small particle of matter in the center known as the nucleus. But the Double-Slit Experiment has revealed that even the nucleus of an atom, just like electrons, pops in and out of existence depending on whether or not someone is looking at it.

This experiment has been repeated numerous times by physicists around the world, and when done correctly, it always produces the same results. This experiment does not only apply to electrons, but it applies to everything at every scale. Even whole atoms and molecules pop in and out of existence. Electrons are relatively easy to use for the experiment, but physicists have also performed the experiment with things like large balls of sixty carbon atoms called Buckminsterfullerene. The more physicists continue to study the way the Universe behaves at the quantum scale, the less solid and real the Universe appears to be.

All matter—everything that we perceive to be solid and real—exists as waves, and the waves only manifest as particles in space and time when we observe them, showing clearly that there is no reality independent of the observer, no reality independent of Consciousness.

Without Consciousness, there can be nothing to be conscious of. On the same token, without something to be conscious of, Consciousness cannot know that it exists. How can there be an observer without something to observe? And how can something be observed without an observer?

Earlier, we were able to divide the Universe into subject and object, and this is a very useful practice when it comes to reconnecting with your subjective awareness. But in Truth, subject and object are not separate—so-called objective reality is projected by our subjective Consciousness. Reality is not something that exists "out there" independent of Consciousness; it is something that Consciousness projects based on the information it obtains from "The Implicate Order"—it is something that exists within us.

Subject and object are one. There can be no perception without an object of perception, and the object of perception is not separate from the one who is perceiving. Right now these words appear to be outside of you, but that is not true. They are the object of your perception—right now, they are you.

When we perceive the stars, the stars are the object of our perception—they exist within us. When we perceive the ocean, the ocean is also within us. The idea that things exist outside of our Consciousness is an illusion. Ancient wisdom traditions have known this for centuries, and even modern science has recognized that our sense organs merely receive information and project it within our own minds. Vision does not take place in the eye, but in an area located in the back of the brain. Everything that we perceive to be "out there" is being experienced "in here."

"Although mind and objects are considered two different fields, in fact, they are one. Mind is the perceiver and objects of mind are the perceived. But perceiver and perceived can never be separated; they make one whole. Objects of mind do not arise independently of mind. Objects of mind—including the body, the feelings, and all other mental formations—are products of mind."

— Thich Nhat Hanh

This concept is often difficult to grasp because it is completely contradictory to the common belief of our culture. As mentioned before, our beliefs shape how we perceive reality to be, and the belief that shapes our current perception of reality was adopted by the worldview of Newtonian physics, which asserts that reality is objective—that there is a material universe existing outside of our experience. But this isn't true; there is no material universe outside of you; the Universe takes form through you.

So-called objective reality and subjective experience are not two separate things. This is the fundamental Truth that philosophies like Advaita Vedanta have known for millennia.

Advaita is a Sanskrit word meaning "nondual" and Vedanta refers to the ancient Hindu texts called "The Vedas." The Sanskrit word Veda translates as knowledge, and the word Anta translates as end. Therefore, Vedanta is the end of knowledge—the realization that reality is nondual.

Vedic philosophers use the word nondual, rather than one, because one implies two, and nondual suggests there are not two. What we perceive to be objective reality is really a projected image that our minds create. In other words, we project images of reality within our minds that appear to be outside of us.

Believing that things really are outside of us, rather than being projections of our own minds, is what ancient wisdom traditions have commonly referred to as delusion, or ignorance. This is the fundamental delusion that Zen Master Yasutani Roshi spoke of when he said, *"The fundamental delusion of humanity is to suppose that I am here and you are there."* Reality is not something that exists independent of our minds; rather it is something that our minds project.

When physicists speak of an electron existing as a wave, it isn't like an ocean or radio wave, but rather a wave of potential locations where the electron could end up as a particle once it is observed—a wave of possibilities. The way that physicist Nick Herbert explains it is that behind your back, the world is a flowing, amorphous quantum soup. But the moment you turn and try to see the soup, your glance turns it back into our ordinary, everyday reality. This quantum soup—this wave of possibilities from which all matter arises, and what David Bohm called "The Implicate Order"—has also been given many other names such as "The Unified Field," "The Quantum Field," "The Zero Point Field," "The Quantum Wave Function," and "The Planck Scale," to name a few.

"The Field" is a field of infinite possibilities out of which everything is created. It is a place outside of space and time where everything, all possibilities, already exist, but only in waveform. This field does not contain particles or matter, and is not a part of the physical Universe. Rather, it is what the entire Universe is made from.

The problem is that since The Field exists outside of space and time, its existence cannot be proven by our standard scientific methods. It cannot be observed, it cannot be measured, for the very act of observing or measuring causes the field to pop out of its wave state and manifest as particles in space and time.

However, when quantum physicists assume that The Field is there, they are able to make astonishingly accurate mathematical predictions about the physical Universe and how it behaves. In this way, it is similar to electricity. You cannot see electricity itself, but only what electricity produces, and when we see the effects of electricity, we know that it exists. There are actually no fields that we can perceive directly with our ordinary senses—whether its gravity, electromagnetism, or information. We only perceive the effects that fields produce, not the fields themselves.

Based on the information that quantum physics is providing, it seems as if physicists are reaffirming what ancient wisdom traditions have said for thousands of years—that objective reality is an illusion, and that the true reality is subjective. Physicists are beginning to sound more and more like metaphysicists and shamans in their way of viewing the world.

In Hinduism, this Quantum Field has been given the name Akasha. Akasha—also referred to as the Akashic Field, or Akashic Record—is described as a field beyond space and time from which everything emerges. Both Hindu philosophy and quantum theory suggest that the observed world is only a manifestation of this deeper dimension.

Hindu cosmology states that there are five elements in the Universe—Earth, Water, Fire, Air, and Akasha—Akasha being the fundamental element. Akasha holds the other elements in itself, but it is also outside of them, for it is beyond both space and time. Paramahansa Yogananda describes Akasha as the subtle background against which everything in the material universe becomes perceptible.

According to the great yogi Swami Vivekananda, Akasha is: *"the omnipresent, all-penetrating existence. Everything that has form, everything that is the result of combination, is evolved out of this Akasha. It is the Akasha that becomes the air, that becomes the liquids, that becomes the solids; it is the Akasha that becomes the sun, the earth, the moon, the stars, the comets; it is the Akasha that becomes the human body, the animal body, the plants, every form that we see, everything that can be sensed, everything that exists. It cannot be perceived; it is so subtle that it is beyond all ordinary perception; it can only be seen when it has become gross, has taken form. At the beginning of creation there is only this Akasha. At the end of the cycle the solid, the liquids, and the gases all melt into the Akasha again, and the next creation similarly proceeds out of this Akasha"*

Akasha is the Quantum Field that exists prior to space and time; it is the fundamental matrix in which all things arise, through which all things exist, and into which all things return. According to both Hindu cosmology and quantum physics, the world we experience is not the ultimate reality; it is only a manifestation of that reality.

"This is not the real reality.
The real reality is behind the curtain.
In truth, we are not here.
This is our shadow."

– Rumi, 13th Century Poet

The Answer Is YOU

8   The Holographic Universe

If all possibilities already exist within The Field, and the reality we experience is manifested out of The Field, you may be wondering why we continue to experience a reality that is relatively the same each time it is manifested. This is due to the probability that The Field will manifest as a particular reality once observed.

The Double-Slit Experiment shows that what makes anything come into material existence is an accessible record of that thing existing in some particular way. Without that recorded data, the thing only exists as a probability. Once the record is made, the record of that thing existing a certain way means it must exist that way for as long as the record is available in the universe. This allows for a consistent reality to be manifested each time it is observed.

Another experiment that can help us better understand this phenomenon is a variation of The Double-Slit Experiment known as "The Delayed Choice Quantum Eraser Experiment." This experiment was set up to eliminate all variables of The Double-Slit Experiment that scientists have used to propose that the experiment is somehow flawed.

Rather than explaining the actual experiment to you, I will explain a less technical representation of the experiment so that it is easier to comprehend.

In this experiment, we will perform The Double-Slit Experiment 102 times. Each time that we perform the experiment, we print out the results recorded by the electron detectors and put them in an envelope. We also put the photographic plate results in an envelope. We don't look at any of the results from either the electron detectors or the photographic plate, nor do we let any copies of the results exist. We simply perform the experiments and put the results in the envelopes. We then take those two envelopes, put them both in a bigger envelope, and label the big envelope with a number corresponding to its sequence in the 102 experiments.

After collecting the results and sealing all of the envelopes, we open envelopes 1 and 102 to check that the results are the same for both envelopes. Envelopes 1 and 102 show the same results: no interference pattern. Therefore, we know the experiment went as expected—we looked at the recorded data, and it showed that the electrons behaved as particles.

After opening those two envelopes, we have 100 envelopes left. We take the remaining envelopes and lock them up in a high quality safe, then wait one year. After waiting a year, we take the envelopes out of the safe and shuffle them into two piles of 50.

We open all of the envelopes in pile 1 and open up the plate result envelopes. All the plate result envelopes contain the same results: no interference pattern. Then we take all the envelopes in pile 2, pull out the detector result envelopes and burn them. Burning the detector result envelopes erases all of the recorded data from the detector.

This time, when we open the plate result envelopes we see an interference pattern in all 50 envelopes. We changed the plate results of the experiment simply by erasing the detector results.

So in short, you take the data from the electron detectors and you take the data from the photographic plate, but you don't look at the data. If you look at it, you'll see no interference pattern. But if you don't look at it, and then you erase the data from the detectors that says which slit they went through, when you look at the data on the photographic plate you get an interference pattern again.

This experiment reveals that if we have a record of how the electron should behave, it will behave that way each time that it is observed. But without the record, it exists in a state of probability. The results of the experiment weren't viewed until a year later, which means that they were mere probability the whole time.

As strange as this experiment may be, it provides evidence of the Truth that reality is not objective—it is subjective. What we perceive to be objective reality is merely a projection of subjective consciousness. There is no reality "out there" independent of the observer, but rather the observer is responsible for the reality that is produced.

Information is downloaded to our brain in wave frequencies from the Field, where it is converted into particles, and then projected "out there" for us to experience as "reality." And the "reality" that we experience is unique to each of us depending on our unique observation. This would explain why, even though we experience a reality that appears to be objective, none of us experience reality in exactly the same way.

A great metaphor for this phenomenon is described in the Toltec tradition. The Toltecs believe that each of us is living in a "personal dream," and that together our personal dreams make up "the dream of the planet." They suggest that our individual realities influence one another, creating our shared collective reality.

Everything exists as information in a field of infinite possibilities, and it is our Consciousness that renders the information and causes it to appear as the material world. The probability that reality will be rendered—or manifested—in a certain way is dependent on the records of how it has been manifested in the past, as well as which of the potential records our beliefs allow us to manifest, and which they do not.

This is likely why ancient traditions refer to The Field as the Akashic Record, because it contains all of the records in the Universe. Many mystics refer to the Akashic Record as a library in which one can access all information, and many psychics and seers state that we all have our own files within the Akashic Record, and by accessing our files, they can tell us information about our lives that we could not know from our sensory experience of the material world. The Akashic Record is the library of all that ever was—every experience is stored as a record within The Field.

The records within our own minds determine the probability of the reality that we manifest. If we change the records within our minds—change our subconscious beliefs—we change what we believe to be possible, thus changing the potential realities that we may experience.

"What we see depends mainly on what we look for."

— John Lubbock

Physicist David Bohm's theory of The Field, or what he calls the Implicate Order, is based on the premise that everything is connected with everything else, and in principle, any individual element could reveal "detailed information about every other element in the universe." The central underlying theme of Bohm's theory is the "unbroken wholeness of the totality of existence as an undivided flowing movement without borders." This is not unlike the unbroken wholeness that mystics have spoken of for thousands of years.

Bohm and other physicists have interpreted the implications of these findings by suggesting that the Universe is really like a giant hologram, and that the reality we experience is not at all how we have believed it to be, but rather it resembles that of a virtual reality. I would like to mention that this is of course a metaphor for something much greater. Nonetheless, based on the new findings in quantum physics, this metaphor may be the best way of explaining the strange and fascinating world in which we live.

The Merriam-Webster definition of a hologram is: "a three-dimensional image reproduced from a pattern of interference produced by a split coherent beam of radiation (as a laser)." In other words, a hologram is a virtual image that is projected by shooting a laser on a two-dimensional piece of film—a piece of film that already contains the projected image in wave-form.

To produce a virtual—or holographic—image, one must first shoot a laser beam out of a laser gun, then immediately split that beam into two beams using a beam splitter. One of the beams—called the reference beam—makes its way along a series of mirrors, eventually hitting a sensitive holographic plate, or film—similar to the film that was used in cameras before digital photography. The other laser beam hits an object first, for example an apple, and then hits the holographic film.

When these two parts of the original laser beam come back together at the holographic film, they interfere with each other just like the waves in the Double-Slit Experiment, forming an interference pattern on the two-dimensional piece of film.

Then, another beam focuses on the film where the apple sits in waveform, and once illuminated by the laser, out pops a virtual image of the apple from the holographic film. The apple appears to be real and solid—it appears to have an extension in space—but if you were to try to touch it, your hand would go right through it.

The process of creating a virtual image is relatively easy to understand, but the idea that reality itself may be virtual—may be a type of hologram—is not so easy to accept. As strange as this may seem, this is what many highly respected quantum physicists are telling us. They claim that based on the latest research, we are living in a type of hologram—that our reality is a virtual image, an illusion that isn't real. It only appears real to us within the hologram.

"Despite its apparent solidity, the universe is at heart a phantasm – a gigantic and splendidly detailed hologram."

– David Bohm, Theoretical Physicist

Everything we see and experience—everything we call our three-dimensional reality—is a projection of information contained within the two-dimensional reality of The Field.

The projected three-dimensionality of such images is not the only remarkable characteristic of holograms. If a hologram of an apple is cut in half and then illuminated by a laser, each half will still be found to contain the entire image of the apple. In fact, even if the halves are divided again, each snippet of film will always be found to contain a smaller but intact version of the original image. Unlike normal photographs, every part of a hologram contains all the information possessed by the whole.

The "whole in every part" nature of a hologram is similar to what ancient wisdom traditions have spoken of for millennia—that, "the one is in the all, and the all is in the one." In Mahayana Buddhism, the holographic nature of reality is explained as Indra's net of jewels. Indra is a deity in Hinduism, Buddhism, and Jainism, and his net of jewels can be thought of as a spider web with dewdrops on it, in which each of the dewdrops contains a reflection of all the other drops.

According to Buddhist mythology, within this vast net there lies a jewel at each juncture. Each jewel represents an individual life form, atom, cell, or unit of Consciousness, and each jewel reflects all the other jewels in this cosmic matrix. In turn, each jewel is intrinsically and intimately connected to all others. Thus, a change in one jewel is reflected in every other jewel.

In the "Avatamsaka Sutra," a student asks a teacher: "*How can all these jewels be considered one jewel?*" The teacher replies by saying, "*If you don't believe that one jewel is all the jewels, just put a dot on the jewel. When one jewel is dotted, there are dots on all the jewels. Since there are dots on all the jewels, we know that all the jewels are one jewel.*"

The moral of Indra's net refers to the ripple of effects that stem from our actions. If we perform a compassionate and loving act, that action will reverberate throughout the universe for eternity. Likewise, we cannot damage one strand of the web without damaging others, and consequently the web as a whole.

In his book, "The Tao of Physics" author Fritjof Capra writes: *"Particles are dynamically composed of one another in a self-consistent way, and in that sense can be said to 'contain' one another. In Mahayana Buddhism, a very similar notion is applied to the whole universe. This cosmic network of interpenetrating things is illustrated in the "Avatamsaka Sutra" by the metaphor of Indra's net, a vast network of precious gems hanging over the palace of the god Indra."*

In the words of Sir Charles Elliot: *"In the Heaven of Indra, there is said to be a network of pearls, so arranged that if you look at one you see all the others reflected in it. In the same way, each object in the world is not merely itself but involves every other object and in fact is everything else. In every particle of dust, there are present Buddhas without number."*

It is not only in Buddhist mythology that the holographic nature of reality is recognized. In the Hermetic philosophy of Ancient Egypt and Greece, this phenomenon is referred to as "The Principle of Correspondence," which states that: "there is always a correspondence between the laws and phenomena of the various planes of Being and Life." Or as the old Hermetic axiom says: "As above, so below; as below, so above."

More evidence to confirm the holographic nature of reality comes from the discovery of what has been commonly termed as "fractals." A fractal is defined as: "a curve or geometric figure, each part of which has the same statistical character as the whole. Fractals are useful in modeling structures (such as eroded coastlines or snowflakes) in which similar patterns recur at progressively smaller scales, and in describing partly random or chaotic phenomena such as crystal growth, fluid turbulence, and galaxy formation."

The discovery of fractals has drawn attention to the fact that the Universe follows similar geometric laws at every scale of reality. It points out that the seemingly large scales of reality are reflections of the seemingly small, and vice-versa—that the microcosm can be found in the macrocosm, and the macrocosm within the microcosm.

Examples of fractals are everywhere in nature. They can be found in the patterns of trees, branches, and ferns, in which each part appears to be a smaller image of the whole. They are found in the branch-like patterns of river systems, lightning, and blood vessels. They can be seen in snowflakes, seashells, crystals, and mountain ranges. We can even see the holographic and fractal-like nature of reality in the structure of the Universe itself, as the clusters of galaxies and dark matter resemble the neurons in our brain, the mycelium network of fungi, as well as the network of the man-made Internet.

All of Nature follows perfectly geometric laws. The Ancient Egyptian, Greek, Peruvian, Mayan, and Chinese cultures were well aware of this, as Phi—known as the Golden Ratio or Golden Mean—was used in the constructions of their sculptures and architecture.

Phi is a number approximately equal to 1.618, when the ratio of length to width is 1.618 to 1, and this ratio is found throughout all of Nature. It is the ratio of the line segments that result when a line is divided in a certain and peculiar way. Say that the total length of a line is 1.618 inches—we will call this "Line A." We then cut "Line A" into two lines—"Line B" and "Line C." Line B is ~1.07867 inches long, and Line C is ~0.5393 inches long. Together, Line B and C make up line A. This is the Phi ratio, and it repeats indefinitely throughout Nature.

You can find Phi throughout the human body, in plants, in DNA, in the solar system, in art and architecture, in music, population growth, and even in the stock market. You can easily observe an example of the Phi ratio in your finger. Taking a look at your index finger, you will see that each section of your index finger, from the tip to the base of the wrist, is larger than the preceding one by about the Phi ratio of 1.618.

In the 12th century, Leonardo Fibonacci wrote in Liber Abaci of a simple numerical sequence that is the foundation for an incredible mathematical relationship behind Phi. This sequence was known as early as the 6th century by Indian mathematicians, and perhaps even sooner by other ancient cultures, but it was Leonardo Fibonacci who introduced it to the west, which is why this sequence is commonly known today as "The Fibonacci Sequence."

Starting with 0 and 1, each new number in the sequence is simply the sum of the two before it: 0, 1, 1, 2, 3, 5, 8, 13, 21, 34, 55, 89, 144… The ratio of each successive pair of numbers in the sequence approximates Phi (1.618…), as 5 divided by 3 is 1.666, and 8 divided by 5 is 1.60.

According to this scale, your fingernail is 1 unit in length, the sum of 1 plus 1 is 2, the sum of 1 plus 2 is 3, the sum of 2 plus 3 is 5, and so on, showing the Fibonacci Sequence in the pattern of growth apparent in your finger. Now, if you curl your hand into a fist, you will notice that your hand makes a spiral, starting from the tip of your index finger out toward the tip of your thumb.

This spiral is formed due to the Fibonacci Sequence, and it is the sequence which is apparent in all of the spirals in nature, from your hand, to your ear, to sea shells, to plants, to trees, to weather patterns, and even entire galaxies. Everywhere in nature Phi and the Fibonacci Sequence can be found.

These geometric patterns display the holographic nature of reality. They show that the Universe follows similar patterns of growth on every scale, that the whole can be reflected in the part and the part in the whole. They give us proof that Nature is not chaotic and random, but that it follows natural laws—patterns of information that imply order, not chaos.

The Holographic Universe

The discovery of geometric patterns like fractals have allowed for huge advancements in the field of computer generated images, and they can give us insight into the computer-like nature of our own reality. According to the discoveries in quantum physics, physicists are now implying that the holographic-like nature of the Universe suggests we are living in a virtual reality.

There is even a new field of physics that has emerged known as "digital physics" which is based on the premise that the Universe is describable by information, and is thus virtual. Digital physics supports the theory that things are not really things—they are data. Physical things can't be waves and particles, but processing can spread like a wave and reboot like a particle.

As we saw in the case of the Delayed Choice Quantum Eraser Experiment, how the Universe is rendered depends on the records within The Field. Erase records from the past and it changes the records of the present.

Some convincing evidence that the Universe is virtual comes from the discovery that our Universe has a beginning, which implies that it must come from somewhere beyond itself, which would make sense in a virtual reality. According to the Big Bang theory, the Universe came into existence 13.7 billion years ago. A virtual reality has a boot up that creates its pixels and space-time based on nothing within itself. Seen in this light, the Big Bang could represent the boot up of our particular Universe. Even more evidence that the Universe is virtual, comes from the fact that the more you zoom in on reality, the more pixelated reality appears to be.

Mainstream science currently views everything as a continual evolution of physical processes, but they have no explanation for how physical processes give rise to subjective experience. This has often been referred to in science as "the hard problem." An objective reality cannot give rise to subjective consciousness, but based on new discoveries in quantum physics, we now know that consciousness can give rise to a reality that is seemingly objective.

A virtual reality cannot compute itself; it needs a computer. According to theories in digital physics, Consciousness is the computer for our Universe. Consciousness is not something produced by the brain or body, but rather the brain is merely a receiver of Consciousness.

This would explain much of the strange phenomena that mainstream science is currently unable to explain, such as the phenomenon of remote viewing, in which people are able to see and accurately describe things that are out of range of the sensory perception of their physical bodies. It would also explain such phenomena as outer-body experiences, or astral travel, in which people report being able to leave their physical bodies and explore different realms of the Universe. It would also make more sense of the mind-over-matter phenomenon of the placebo effect, in which people have been able to heal a range of illnesses, from minor colds to life-threatening diseases, simply through the power of their subconscious beliefs.

According to the worldview of modern science, these types of strange phenomena make no sense, and are usually dismissed without further investigation, even though phenomena of this kind continue to occur, and have been reported by people throughout history. Based on the theory that Consciousness is not a result of physical processes, and is outside of space and time, it would make sense that mind has such a powerful influence over physical reality.

If we can accept that Consciousness is not produced by physical reality, but is rather the computer of our virtual reality, we will also have to acknowledge that since it is not material, it cannot be modeled. This would explain why so many mystics state that the true nature of reality is ultimately unknowable, as it is beyond what is perceptible to us in the physical world. This is described in the ancient text of the Upanishads: *"He who thinks God is not comprehended, by him God is comprehended; But he who thinks that God is comprehended knows him not. God is unknown to those who know him, and is known to those who do not know him at all."*

Consciousness cannot be modeled because it is the computer running the model—the computer running the virtual reality that we call the physical Universe. It cannot be perceived because it is the one perceiving. Thus mind is the primary force in the Universe—matter and energy being secondary.

As conscious beings, we are all tapped into the computing power of the computer computing the Universe, which means ultimately we are the computer. Individual Consciousness is a reflection of Universal Consciousness, and vice-versa. Or, as it is described in the philosophy of Advaita Vedanta: Atman (the individual soul) is Brahman (the universal soul). We are not individual drops in the ocean; we are the entire ocean within a drop. The all is in the one, and the one is in the all, just as the Hermetic Principle of Correspondence suggests.

Another interesting Hermetic Principle found in "The Kyballion" is the Principle of Mentalism, which states that "THE ALL IS MIND; The Universe is Mental." According to a direct quote from "The Kyballion":

"This principle embodies the truth that "All is Mind." It explains that the ALL (which is the substantial reality underlying all the outward manifestations and appearances which we know under the terms of "the material universe," the "phenomena of life," "matter," "energy," and, in short, all that is apparent to our material senses) is SPIRIT which in itself is UNKNOWABLE and UNDEFINABLE, but which may be considered and thought of as AN UNIVERSAL, INFINITE, LIVING MIND. It also explains that all the phenomenal world or universe is simply a Mental Creation of THE ALL, subject to the Laws of Created Things, and that the universe, as a whole, and in its parts or units, has its existence in the mind of THE ALL."

We are not our physical bodies, but rather we are units of Consciousness, a part of the one Universal Consciousness. Our bodies are merely avatars that Consciousness can use to maneuver through the virtual reality of our universe. As Alan Watts eloquently puts it: *"Through our eyes, the universe is perceiving itself. Through our ears, the universe is listening to its harmonies. We are the witnesses through which the universe becomes conscious of its glory, of its magnificence."*

It is clear to us that a video game world is fictional, but to the characters within the video game world, it appears just as solid as our Universe does to us. This is because the characters must follow the established rule-set of that reality. In our reality, the many laws of Nature can be seen as our established rule-set.

A great example of this can be explained in the game of checkers. Checkers is a simple game with a set of rules, nonetheless the number of legal positions checkers can take on a checkerboard is over 10^{20}, that's 100 times more positions than the estimated amount of all the grains of sand on earth; 10^{20} legal positions means that there are 10^{40} possible choices or moves that the players can possibly make.

Chess, a more complex game than checkers, has over 10^{43} possible legal positions, which means there are around 10^{120} possible moves that players can make. Just think of the game of life, which is much more complex, the possible choices we can make within the rule-set of this reality are seemingly infinite.

Checkers and chess are deterministic in that they both offer a limited number of choices, but chess and checkers are nondeterministic in that they facilitate the free will of the players within the limited number of choices.

Our virtual reality, with its established rule-sets (most of which are still a complete mystery), gives Consciousness a world in which it can freely move and explore. Without the rule-set of the game, there would be no foundation on which the game of life could be played. And while the game of life appears to have many different players in it, we are all contained within the "MIND OF THE ALL," within the computer of Consciousness. In Truth, there is really only one player—Consciousness—interacting with and experiencing itself.

"The Universe is a dream dreamed by a single dreamer where all the dream characters dream too."

— Arthur Schopenhauer, 19th Century Philosopher

---

9 Maya

Have you ever had a dream that you were certain was real, only to wake up and realize that everyone and everything in the dream was really you? Well this is how many mystics describe the nature of our reality, as a dream in which we think we are individual personalities existing in the physical universe. But eventually, like in all dreams, we will wake up. Except in this dream we do not wake up to realize we are still in the world, we awake from the world to realize that we are God.

In Advaita Vedanta, and in many other ancient wisdom traditions, the world is said to be an illusion. This illusion is commonly referred to as *maya*, a Sanskrit name which refers to the apparent, or objective reality which is superimposed on the ultimate reality in order to generate the phenomena of what we call the material world. *Maya* is the magic by which we create duality—by which we create two worlds from one. This creation is an illusory creation—it is not real—it is an imaginary manifestation of the one Universal Consciousness, appearing as all of the various phenomena in objective reality. *Maya* is God's, or Consciousness's, creative power of emptying or reflecting itself into all things and thus creating all things—the power of subjectivity to take on objective appearance.

It is interesting to note that the word *maya* is derived from the Sanskrit root *matr*, which means, "to measure, form, build, or lay out a plan." From this root we get such English words as meter, matrix, material, or matter. So the world of *maya*, is simply the world of measurement—of mental and symbolic conventions that divide the Universe. It is also the world of matter, for as we have seen, material things are a product of our mental measuring and dividing which, if mistaken for the ultimate reality, are indeed nothing but illusions.

According to the Hindu tradition, we suffer because we have mistakenly identified our true nature with *maya*, with the contents of the dream, rather than as the dreamer creating the dream. We suffer because we think that we really are these bodies, that we really are our personalities and our individual identities. But these are only illusions, are only apparently, or relatively real. They are not the Truth of who we are.

Many people are closed off from the idea that the world is an illusion. We can sense the world—see it, hear it, taste it, touch it, smell it—and it is all we have ever known from the moment of our birth, so how can this world be an illusion? It is an illusion because it exists solely in our minds. It is created by our Consciousness and our senses.

The world exists because your mind exists. If your mind didn't exist, there would be no world. As you look at these words, you see them in what appears to be a reality outside of you. What you are really seeing is the image that your mind is creating from the electrical signals being sent to your brain. While they may appear to be outside of you, this is an illusion, they exist within your own mind, and are being projected to appear as if they are outside of you. This apparent reality that is projected by our minds, is *maya*, and to believe that *maya* is the ultimate reality is a result of ignorance, or *avidya* in Sanskrit.

The point, then, is not to confuse the world as it is with the world as it is measured into space, time, objects, limits, categories, or concepts of any kind, simply because all measurement is a product of thought, not reality. Just as a tree is not composed of feet and inches, but is conventionally or mentally divided into these units of measurement, so the world is not actually composed of separate things, but appears to be when viewed through the illusion of measurement, or *maya*.

There is an age-old story that describes the nature of *maya*: One evening, a man was traveling home on a narrow county path. The sun was setting and it was becoming dark quite quickly. As the man walked along in the dim light of the setting sun, he saw something in his path ahead. Unable to make it out, he proceeded with caution. The object was long, thin, and slightly coiled. "Snake!" thought the man as he stopped dead in his tracks. The man, while in fear of the snake, knew that this was his only way home. Having some fire tools, he quickly fashioned a torch and proceeded carefully forward. As he did, the dangerous snake revealed itself to be merely a rope. With this realization, the man exhaled a sigh of relief, and became aware of how quickly fear became relaxation, panic became peace, and how his mind had been deceived by what his senses had perceived.

This story points out the way in which our senses can so easily deceive us, and seems to suggest that once we perceive things as they really are, such as perceiving the rope to really be just a rope, our fear and suffering can cease. Once we are no longer ignorant and instead have true knowledge of reality, there is no need to be afraid, and we are free to continue on our way.

Like the man in the story afraid of what he had mistaken for a snake, the world of human beings is trembling under a misconception of what they have mistaken for reality. The world of appearances may exist, but it is an illusion. Just as the true nature of the snake in the story was really a rope, the true nature of illusion in our story is really the pure and absolute Consciousness. All things are superimposed on this eternal, unchanging, free, transcendent, timeless, and spaceless Awareness which is your true nature. You are and have always been this one universal awareness, even if you have forgotten your true Self in the world of *maya*—in the illusion of being "me," "my body," "my personality," "my experience," and "my story"—all of which are merely illusions of the mind.

Can you recall a time in which you were at peace, only for something in your experience to disturb your peace and cause you to experience a strong sense of anger or irritation? Can you see how the thoughts in your mind completely shifted the reality that you were experiencing? This is because reality has its source in your mind. The world changes according to your mind, your perceptions, your preoccupations, your desires, and your interests.

Many people experience the world, but their experiences are not the same as yours. They experience a reality that changes according to their own minds, their own perceptions, their own interactions, their own beliefs, their own circumstances, and their own interests. Reality keeps on changing according to how you perceive it, and exists in your mind as an object. This reality that appears to be objective is in fact subjective; it is an illusion that operates in relation to our senses.

"Reality is merely an illusion, albeit a very persistent one."
– Albert Einstein, Theoretical Physicist

The Answer Is YOU

10 The Play of God

The concept of *maya*, explains that reality is an illusion, experienced uniquely to each of the conscious beings that are a part of the one cosmic Consciousness, but it does not explain why this illusion exists. The answer to this question can be found in another Hindu concept, and this is the concept of *Lila*, or *Leela*, a Sanskrit word that can be roughly translated as "play." *Lila* is the play of God, a theatre, or game, in which God can create, live, and express Itself. This divine play is obviously a mythical description of the way things are, and is not exactly as they are. Nonetheless, it is perhaps one of the most satisfactory explanations for answering the question of why the Universe was created.

Being just pure Consciousness, if it were possible, would be quite boring. It would be like staring at a blank wall for all of eternity. Thus, the creation of various conscious beings is for the purpose of enjoyment—to have something to witness. Only through the interaction with universal energy can universal consciousness know that it exists. For universal Consciousness, creation is like a mirror, the only image it can get of itself—even if the image is not a totally complete reflection.

The Ancient Hindu scripture of the Chandogya Upanishad states: "*Sarvam Khalvidam Brahma*" meaning, "Everything is Brahman" or, "Everything is God." The multiplicities of the world are not separate from God, they only appear to be separate from God. In Truth, they are God. All things have their origin in God, are sustained in God, and return to God.

According to the concept of *Lila*, God created this world for the purpose of enjoyment, but He (or She, or It) is not separate from the world that was created. God and the world—the creator and the created—are not two distinct separate things, but are one and the same. Life is an interactive theatre in which everyone is both the actor and the spectator, energy and consciousness.

Of course, these are only words and concepts, and they can never describe the essence of life in its entirety. But is it not the desire for experience that lies at the base of your every action? Whatever the result of any action is, is it not something you wish to experience? And do you not always seek enjoyment from that experience? We can see that enjoyment is the driving force in our own lives, and we can consider that it would be the same for God, the universal witness. But if the purpose of creation was for enjoyment, why is there so much suffering in the world? Why is there so much destruction, chaos, and misery?

The Play of God

Imagine for a moment that life really was just a play. Could you imagine what it would be like to witness a play in which every actor played the role of someone who knew it was only a play? That would not be much fun would it? In fact it would likely ruin the entire play. So the delusion of *maya*, of being the actor, of being an entity that exists apart from God, is essential in order for the game of life to be truly entertaining.

How would a person ever grow to maturity if they did not have the desires and ambitions that come from feeling one is an individual? The actors need to take their roles seriously in order for the play to be truly enjoyable. This is why consciousness takes on various personalities and identifies with the various forms that it inhabits—to forget itself in the role of the play.

Then what use is enlightenment if delusion is required to play the game? As in all games, once one level is completed, only the next level brings enjoyment. Enlightenment is simply the final level of the game of life— the final act of the play in which Consciousness, after losing itself in the world, once again discovers itself as the Infinite Creator of the play.

According to the philosophy of *Lila*, God creates the world by an act of self-dismemberment, or self-forgetting, whereby the one becomes many, and the single actor plays innumerable parts. By this act of self-dismemberment, God becomes all beings, yet at the same time never ceases to be God. And in the end, God comes back to find himself—the one dying into the many, and the many dying into the one.

In his book "The Book On the Taboo Against Knowing Who You Are," Alan Watts describes the play of *Lila* as a game of hide and seek: "*God also likes to play hide-and-seek, but because there is nothing outside of God, he has no one but himself to play with. But he gets over this difficulty by pretending that he is not himself. This is his way of hiding from himself. He pretends that he is you and I and all the people in the world, all the animals, all the plants, all the rocks, and all the stars. In this way he has strange and wonderful adventures, some of which are terrible and frightening. But these are just like bad dreams, for when he wakes up they will disappear.*"

He goes on to say: "*Now when God plays hide and pretends that he is you and I, he does it so well that it takes him a long time to remember where and how he hid himself. But that's the whole fun of it—just what he wanted to do. He doesn't want to find himself too quickly, for that would spoil the game. That is why it is so difficult for you and me to find out that we are God in disguise, pretending not to be himself. But when the game has gone on long enough, all of us will wake up, stop pretending, and remember that we are all one single Self—the God who is all that there is and who lives for ever and ever.*"

While there may be suffering, pain, and misery in the world, this is all a part of the drama of the play. And it is this drama that brings excitement, challenge, and intensity to the play of life. Pleasure cannot be appreciated when pain is unknown. Food is only satisfying to one who is hungry. Black can only be perceived alongside the contrast of white. It is this contrast in life which gives life its meaning, its depth, and its purpose.

The Play of God

It is important to remember that the real you, the observer of the play, is never affected by what happens to the actor. You are simply witnessing the play that you yourself are performing. God is not creating a game for us to suffer and play in. God is not sitting somewhere out there enjoying the show. God is playing the game all by himself, and his suffering and enjoyment are also yours, because you are him/her/it.

God is the ultimate ground of Being, and this ultimate ground of Being is YOU. For one who realizes their true nature as God, as Consciousness, life becomes a joy without end. Then love flows like a powerful wave toward all of the fellow actors within the play, simply because all of the other actors are YOU, playing a different part in this cosmic play.

How can there be anything but love felt for another who is but a reflection of oneself? How can one feel sadness for what is lost, only for it to return in some form or another? How can one have fear of losing anything when they realize that they are everything? When all of those fears and undesirable emotions dissolve in the ocean of your loving awareness, then Love becomes your very Being.

But as long as one does not realize their formless nature as Consciousness, these negative feelings will still arise through attachment to the impermanent and ever-changing forms of the world. Like children, we so easily forget that we are just playing a game. Whether we win or lose the game doesn't matter. The only thing that matters is that we play the game.

The real you can never really suffer, can never really be sad, miserable, or afraid—because the real you is eternally blissful, ever at rest, ever at peace. When you realize fully your formless nature, and your oneness with existence, and are no longer fooled by the ever-changing forms of the material world, then you have reached the state of enlightenment, the final level of the game of life.

Then you have true freedom—the freedom to be, the freedom to live life without being bound to it, the freedom to experience gain and loss without suffering from gain or loss. You are eternal, infinite, and formless Consciousness, dancing with the ever-changing and impermanent world of form. You can withdraw from this world or you can embrace it. But God did not create the world just for everyone to try to escape it. The true purpose of life is to enjoy the creation, in whatever form it manifests.

This is why the Tantric approach to enlightenment is focused on embracing life, enjoying the illusions and the play of the divine, not resisting it or denying it like many traditions encourage a seeker to do.

In our experience, there is both the ever-changing world of form, and there is the never changing world of the formless. The world of form is the world created by our senses, the world of illusion, or *maya*, that we are so familiar with. The formless is what this sensory based world takes place in—Consciousness. Most of our suffering comes from identifying with the world of form, and forgetting our formless nature. This is why so many traditions proclaim

The Play of God

that one should renounce the world and retreat within themselves to discover their nature as the formless.

While this may help one discover their formless nature, it only shifts identification from the form to the formless, and identifying with either one by itself causes one to miss out on the other. So many people that have been led to a spiritual path think that enlightenment will come from escaping the world, but this takes all of the enjoyment out of life—which is why life was created in the first place.

The world of form may be an illusion, may be only relatively true, and is not the absolute Truth, but it still exists, so why resist it? Why not embrace life, embrace the world of form, embrace this cosmic play, experience the many joys that life has to offer, all while remembering that YOU, as the one formless Consciousness, are always the free and peaceful witness of this divine creation.

It is important to remember that everything in your experience is also another aspect of YOU. The formless Consciousness lies at the center of every form, you are always experiencing yourself, in whatever form your Consciousness is manifesting. It is you who is reading these words, and it is also you who is writing them. My Consciousness and your Consciousness, while apparently different, are really one and the same.

The formless and the form are not two separate things, or as the Buddha said, *"Emptiness is form, and form is emptiness."* You are the form and formless both. You are everything that is. Life may be an illusion, but it is a beautiful illusion in which you can experience the beauty of creation, the artwork of nature, the light and warmth of the sun, the energy and spirit of the air, the diversity of life on earth, and the many magical things that this world has to offer. All are divine expressions of the totality that is YOU—everything is an extension of you, just as you are an extension of everything.

"The entire Universe is God's cosmic motion picture, and that individuals are merely actors in the divine play who change roles through reincarnation; mankind's deep suffering is rooted in identifying too closely with one's current role, rather than with the movie's director, or God."

– Paramahansa Yogananda

---

11 Shiva & Shakti

There is a Tantric philosophy that beautifully describes your existence as both the form and the formless, and can be seen as a poetic explanation for some of the mindboggling theories of quantum physics. This philosophy is the divine dance of Shiva and Shakti.

What physicists call, "The Quantum Field" and what Hindus call Akasha, is the matrix of information that the energy of the Universe emerges from. In the Tantric tradition, this essential Energy is referred to as Shakti—the Mother Goddess—seen as the feminine principle of the Universe. It is the one Energy that takes all shapes and forms, that makes up the illusion of *maya*, and allows for our experience of the material world. Shiva is one of the Hindu names for Consciousness—the Creator—seen as the masculine principle of the Universe. Just like Shiva, the essential energy of Shakti can be found in all of the manifested Universe.

Everything that we experience—all of the forms of the material world—are Shakti, the feminine principle. This has nothing to do with gender in the conventional sense; it applies solely to energy. Feminine energy is that which makes the non-manifest manifest; what brings the formless into form. Everything exists through this feminine force, but emerges out of nonexistence—out of Consciousness—the masculine principle. Feminine and masculine—Energy and Consciousness—are not separate; they exist in union.

Without you as Consciousness, this universal Energy cannot be experienced; and without the Energy, Consciousness cannot even indirectly experience itself. Neither Consciousness nor Energy have existence by and of themselves—there exists only the experience, or *beingness*, which requires both and includes both, a subject and an object, an observer and a thing to observe.

This universal Energy can only emerge from your witnessing, and this essential Energy is also you, a natural attribute of the Universe that is as eternal as you are. Even modern science recognizes this fact, as the first law of thermodynamics is the law of conservation of energy, which states that: "*the total energy of an isolated system is constant; energy can be transformed from one form to another, but cannot be created or destroyed.*" Shiva and Shakti—Consciousness and Energy— are not two separate things. They are not entirely the same, nor are they not the same. We cannot say exactly what they are. They are two sides of the same coin.

While in the Vedic traditions Brahman, or Consciousness, is said to be something different than Akasha, or the Quantum Field, many quantum physicists do not agree with this, but instead proclaim that what we call the Quantum Field *is* our Consciousness—it is a field that consists of quantum possibilities for the manifestation of consciousness itself. Either way that we choose to look at it, Consciousness and The Field, Brahman and Akasha, Shiva and Shakti, are ultimately inseparable.

The Divine, while depicted as the Father in many religions, is not separate from the Mother. God is both masculine and feminine—God and Goddess; Consciousness and Energy. You too have both feminine and masculine qualities within your own being, regardless of your physical gender. Much of the suffering in our world today comes from suppressing our feminine aspect, and overemphasizing the masculine, thus creating a huge imbalance within us.

The masculine is often portrayed as that which is strong, logical, rational, hard, active, competitive, providing, and outspoken. While the feminine is portrayed as that which is gentle, emotional, intuitive, soft, passive, cooperative, nurturing, and quiet. In our male-dominant culture, many of us are out of tune with our femininity, and suffer because we have not developed the sensitivity to feel our emotions, to allow ourselves to be vulnerable, and to trust our intuition rather than rational thinking.

Vulnerability is often seen as a sign of weakness, but it takes true strength to allow oneself to be open; much more strength than it takes to close oneself off. We must learn to balance both masculine and feminine qualities within us, and reconnect with the qualities of our being that have been suppressed.

This is a fundamental truth recognized in many different cultures. It is also one of the seven Hermetic principles in the Kyballion, the "Principle of Gender," which states that *"Gender is in everything; everything has its Masculine and Feminine Principles; Gender manifests on all planes."*

Regardless of whether you are a man or woman, you contain both masculine and feminine energies within you. Consciousness and Energy—Shiva and Shakti—together are what you are. You cannot be limited to either one of them, even if you naturally identify with Consciousness after seeing beyond the illusions of form.

This still leaves us with a dual definition about ourselves, as being both Consciousness and Energy, the witness and the reality being witnessed. What lies beyond this apparent duality is a state of being that is beyond both—beyond all words, beyond all concepts, beyond all descriptions, definitions, or names, because it is beyond form and beyond the formless as well. It is both Consciousness and Energy, with neither coming first nor dominating the other. This experience of pure being is what mystics have commonly named enlightenment or universal love—it is the divine union of Shiva and Shakti, of masculine and feminine, of yang and yin, of Consciousness and Energy.

Enlightenment is seen as the ultimate liberation, it is the freedom from suffering that so many people desire. In Sanskrit, the word for liberation is *moksha*, and the purpose of most Indian traditions is to attain *moksha*, to reach a state in which we are absolutely free from the world of form, but also free to explore it and enjoy it, without our ignorance of our true nature causing us to cling to reality and suffer.

The way to enlightenment is not through rejecting form, but realizing that you are both the form and the formless. Your Energy aspect, by itself, has no Consciousness. So it cannot realize itself, or anything, without the help of your Consciousness. Only Consciousness can realize itself, which is why the search for enlightenment is focused primarily on Consciousness. Though once enlightenment is reached, there is only nondual being, which includes both Energy and Consciousness, though they are no longer experienced as opposites, but are realized as one.

When a being with form realizes its formless nature as Shiva, it looks upon the universal Energy of Shakti from the point of view of cosmic Consciousness. Thus, the universal Energy becomes the beloved, the Shakti of Shiva.

This universal Energy is ever-changing—producing enjoyment and suffering in those who do not realize their formless nature, and so cling to the forms of this changing energy and desire for it to be permanent. But how could life be possible without change? The same change that allows a child to grow into an adult is the same change that causes the adult to eventually grow old and die. The changes that we embrace with joy are the same changes that we resist with fear. Life could not exist without change, without movement, or without growth.

Life is a continuous flow, and by clinging to life we

restrict this flow, and cause ourselves to suffer. Or, as Alan Watts says, *"The desire for security and the feeling of insecurity are the same thing. To hold your breath is to lose your breath."* We cannot grasp life any more than we can grasp the air between our fingers; to enjoy life we must let it flow, in whatever way that it naturally chooses to.

The being who fully realizes their formless nature is no longer fooled by the ever-changing forms of the material world. Thus, the Love for the beloved becomes pure, without any conflict or duality, without any attachment, without desire or expectation.

You are Shiva and Shakti both; but as long as you have not realized your true nature, you will continue to suffer from your confusion of their essential natures. If you believe yourself to be the form of this body, or any of the forms of the manifested Universe that are always changing, then you will remain caught in duality and your happiness will ever change into your unhappiness and back again.

If you want to be free of the suffering caused by this confusion, then you need to realize that the YOU that is experiencing is the Shiva, and that your Consciousness, or Shiva, never changes and is always at peace. Only then will the ever-changing energy of Shakti, who is also you but not you, as the one experiencing, becomes a joy to experience, a pleasure to be with, a beloved to love.

Once you realize that everything is the dance of Shiva and Shakti, you cannot help but feel an overwhelming sense of freedom and love for life, no matter what form it manifests in. Whether it is the form of this body, the people in your life, the beauty of Nature that surrounds you, or even this book—all are your beloved coming to greet you in the ever flowing and ever changing dance of life. Even the seemingly bad things such as war, poverty, and disease, can be looked upon as your beloved.

When you see another being suffering, you realize that it is your beloved who is suffering, and your beloved is you. Within every form lies the formless. All of the manifested Universe has Consciousness at its core. Life is a giant mandala of geometric energy, emerging out of and dancing around the formless and blissful center of consciousness that is YOU. Everything and everyone is your beloved, as everything and everyone is YOU.

The Tantric approach to enlightenment focuses on merging Shakti with Shiva, merging the individual Consciousness with the Universal Consciousness; this is also the purpose of *Yoga*, a Sanskrit word which means "union." Of course the individual and Universal Consciousness were never really separate in the first place; but only appear to be separate to those under the spell of *maya*.

Many other traditions have a similar approach. The Hermetic philosophy understands that the microcosm is a reflection of the macrocosm, and the way to reach the macrocosm is through the microcosm. In other words, the way to reach the universal and cosmic you, is through the individual you.

The Answer Is YOU

12 Conditioning

If we are to understand and fully realize who we are, we must look into the reason why we have become ignorant of our true nature. I think the best way to understand this is through the analogy of comparing our minds to a garden. When we were born, our minds were pure, open, and aware. Our minds were nothing but rich and fertile soil.

Then, as we were exposed to our environment, we were conditioned by the beliefs, concepts, and worldviews of the culture in which we were born. People began planting seeds in the fertile soil of our minds. Whether our mental gardens were planted with seeds of love or fear, peace or violence, knowledge or ignorance, depended on the influence of the people around us.

We adopted our beliefs about what reality is, according to how the other beings in our life perceived reality— according to the beliefs that they have adopted from their own conditioning. These beliefs shape the way in which we perceive our world. They define what we think of ourselves, what we think of reality, and what we think is possible in our reality.

When we were born, we went into what Ram Dass calls "somebody training." We were taught that we are our name, and that we are an individual personality living amongst a world of other individual personalities. Of course we didn't really think much of this when we were children, as our only concern was playing and being. Nonetheless, the seed of individuality and separation was planted in the fertile soil of our minds, and as we grew, this seed was watered with repetition, blossoming into the way that we perceive reality.

As we developed, our senses were flooded with information from our family and our culture, each bit of information planting a seed in our mind's garden. Each time we curiously asked our parents about the nature of something, they answered to the best of their ability, and whatever answer they gave us, planted a seed in the soil of our minds.

We asked the adults around us what "this" was, and what "that" was and so we began defining things and separating them into their own mental labels and boxes: "mom, dad, dog, cat, book, table, chair, etc." and this is the very same language that we continue to use when defining our reality, but we did not create this language, we merely adopted it from our culture.

As children, especially in our modern society, we were also exposed to a vast range of different forms of media— books, music, radio, television, video games—each of which planted their own seeds in our minds, shaping our ideas about reality accordingly.

When we went to school, we began learning about the world from the common perspective of our culture, and this also played a major role in shaping our beliefs about reality. School is perhaps the most detrimental to our freedom, as we are all taught to understand and perceive things in exactly the same way, and if we do not learn what we are taught, we are ridiculed, judged, and even punished.

When we were punished as children, whether it was from our parents, from our siblings, from our teachers, or from anyone, this act of violence traumatized us. We learned not to do what caused us to receive punishment so that we would no longer have to experience the trauma.

Children are very straightforward with what they see, and often what they see is not what the other members in society see. The child is then punished to the point where they don't want to see things in a certain way anymore because it is just too painful. So then they begin seeing things from the view of the social program that everyone wants them to see, so that they will no longer have to experience the pain of being punished.

Aside from the many concepts, ideas, opinions, and beliefs that we adopted throughout our schooling, we also underwent a range of different traumatic experiences. Not only did we receive punishment or pain from adults and authority figures, we received it from the other traumatized children that we were surrounded by on a daily basis.

Children judge and make fun of other children for being different than they are, and it is likely that even you have judged or criticized other children in this way. When a child receives this judgment from one of their peers, they begin to judge themselves, and they change who they are in order to fit in with others, to avoid the pain and trauma of being judged, made fun of, or abused.

In high school, this same social structure leads to one being afraid of being embarrassed. People do not do what they love to do, and are not being who they want to be, because they are afraid that they will be judged by the people around them. This stems from the many traumatic experiences one has been through in their past. They experienced something so personally traumatizing that they would rather be someone who they are not, than be judged, made fun of, or abused for being who they are.

These experiences, no matter how subtle or severe they may be, slowly harden our spirit, and prevent us from being our natural selves. Little by little we are taught to conform to a way of being that is the least offensive, the least different, the least extraordinary, and the least subject to judgment or ridicule.

This process of traumatic experiences and social conditioning often transforms the courageous dreamer one was as a child into a fearful realist that so many people behave as today. Once out of high school, this fear of embarrassment has become so strong, that one often takes a path of following along with the crowd, doing what is expected of them, doing what will involve the least amount of opposition from others, and what will look good in the eyes of society, rather than following their dreams, doing what they love to do, and being who they want to be.

Conditioning

Our social conditioning and cultural programming creates a type of prison for us, where we are bound to stay confined to what society has deemed "normal"—a word that refers to no more than a social class that people must live in or else suffer judgment, ridicule, and punishment for being themselves.

From the moment of birth we are conditioned to fit in with what society views as normal—to share the worldviews and beliefs of our culture. Unfortunately, our culture is operating on the momentum of an ignorant past, and so, perceives things in a way that is not at all in harmony with the truth of reality, but rather conforms to a set of made up beliefs, concepts, and opinions about reality. This has caused us to develop a false understanding of the world, and consequently a false understanding of who we are.

We do not realize our true nature as Consciousness, but rather, we have confused our identity with an idea of ourselves—a mental image projected by Consciousness. This illusory identity is what many refer to as, "the ego." The ego is not who we are, it is who we think we are. It is the identity that we have adopted from our culture—the idea of being a personality that exists separately from the Universe as a whole.

The Answer Is YOU

13 Ego

Why is it that we feel so separate from our environment? Why do we have the strong sensation that the being inside of our skin is somehow separate from the world outside of our skin? We feel that there is intelligence within us, and we can acknowledge the intelligence in others, but we do not look to the Universe at large as if it also possessed this intelligence. Instead, we perceive the Universe as if it were a dull and mechanical thing that somehow gave rise to intelligent life. But as Alan Watts says, *"we did not come into this world, we came out of it, in the same way as a flower comes out of a plant, or a fruit comes out of a tree. And as an apple tree 'apples,' the solar system in which we live, and therefore the galaxy in which we live, and therefore the system of galaxies in which we live—that system 'peoples,' and therefore people are an expression of its energy and of its nature."* Therefore, if there is intelligence within human beings, then the energy that human beings express must also be intelligent.

But the average person does not consider themselves to be an expression of the energy of the total Universe, even though a human being cannot exist except in an environment of earth, water, heat, air, and space. The elements outside of our skin are just as important to us as the elements inside of our skin. We cannot describe ourselves apart from our natural environment, and so, we should realize that our natural environment is an essential part of who we are.

However, this is not how most people feel. Most people feel rather separate from their environment, and according to the common perception of our culture, nature is even seen as a destructive force that we must battle with, conquer, and control if we are to survive. This attitude toward nature has caused a huge amount of destruction to the natural environment and, consequently, is leading to the destruction of human beings as well. There is no force in nature more destructive than a society of human beings who have forgotten their connection to the natural world.

But this idea of being separate from nature is an illusion—we are as much a part of nature as a wave is a part of the ocean. Our ignorance of our connection to nature arises from the limitation that we human beings have in perceiving nature. The conscious awareness of a human being is a kind of linear scanning system, it examines the world bit by bit, just as one can only look upon a dark room with a flashlight by illuminating it one piece at a time.

This is why school takes so many years to complete, because we obtain information about the world by scanning through countless lines of print. But the world does not come at us in lines; it is a multidimensional continuum in which everything everywhere is happening all together at once. We are exposed to far too much information at any given moment to translate the experience into a limited amount of words, symbols, or numbers, as symbols for reality are not reality itself. You cannot eat the word "food," or drink the word "water." In exactly the same way, you cannot define who you are by labeling yourself as "I" or "me."

While using manmade symbols, words, and concepts has proven to be very useful in our society, we have become so fascinated by these measurements of reality, that we have confused the world as it is with the world as it is measured, described, and conceptualized. And when we are not aware of ourselves except for in a symbolic way, we are not really aware of ourselves at all. We are, as Alan Watts says, *"like people eating menus instead of dinners, and that is why we are all psychologically frustrated."*

So what is it that we mean by the word "I"? Well, obviously "I" is simply our symbol of ourselves—a symbol that represents the entire organism of the Universe as it is centered on our individual consciousness—and the symbol is not the real thing.

Our entire culture has become so psychologically obsessed with the world of symbols, of social conventions, of mental divisions and measurements, that we are no longer in touch with the whole of nature—a whole that is so vast, complex, and interconnected that it couldn't possibly be confined to the social conventions of language and symbols.

Because of our confusion of the true nature of reality with reality as it is conceptualized or measured, we have attached our identity to the ego, something that has no basis in physical reality. The ego is essentially a large collection of thoughts, all connected to one singular thought at the center that we call "I" or "me."

When we are confused with the world of measurement, confused with the world of illusion or *maya*, we carry within us this "I" thought that we think we are, and we have many different concepts about ourselves and the way we relate to reality that we attach to this thought. The problem with this is that the "I" thought is really an illusion, and so we feel that we have to constantly protect, defend, and advocate for this illusory identity. So we come up with a wide range of different beliefs, concepts, ideas, and opinions that are mixed in with our conditioning, our traumas, and our various neuroses, in order to protect and steward this illusory thought that we call "I."

As a result of this collection of thoughts—or ego—we feel as though we have a very heavy burden to carry—some identity that we must always watch out for, live up to, and validate to others to prove that it exists in some way or another. We feel that we must always defend our beliefs, our worldviews, our opinions etc., because these make up our sense of identity, and if any of the aspects that we identify with are threatened, on some level we perceive that as a threat to our survival, an attack on who we are.

So the ego can also be thought of as our attachment to form, whether the forms be physical, mental, or emotional. Whatever we attach to—be it our thoughts, our feelings, our body, our name, our profession, our personality, our beliefs, our memories, our accomplishments, our social roles, etc.— are forms that we cling to for a sense of identity, when our true identity is formless, and consists of all things, not any one or few things in particular.

It is because we identify with the ego that we feel the need to force our beliefs and opinions onto others, as a way to validate our own sense of identity. It is because we identify with the ego that we feel we need to show off or lie about our experience in order to improve our social image. It is because we identify with the ego that we desire for the recognition and approval of others. And it is because we identify with the ego that we live in a state of constant fear and worry as a result of feeling the need to protect our identity.

When someone is heavily ego-identified, their behavior becomes a double-sided coin of self-importance and self-pity. They feel that they are special, and of more worth and importance than anyone else. But because they cling to this identity and this need for importance, they also compare themselves to others, and try to outdo everyone and glorify their status and image as an attempt to enforce their need to feel special.

Because they feel they are special and more important than others, they also feel that they should receive special treatment, and when they don't they perceive themselves as victims of their circumstances, when really they are victims of their minds and their way of thinking. "Why me?" is one of the ego's favorite pleas to reinforce its belief that the world revolves around it.

To the person identified with the ego, everything and everyone are seen only in the light of how they can benefit "me." Greed, lust, violence, attachment, judgment, criticism, blame—all are qualities of the ego.

You can very easily recognize the ego within yourself. You can feel when you have an urge to protect your image or reputation, or enforce your beliefs onto another and prove that you are right. Our culture, being one profoundly obsessed with the symbolic and conceptual representations of reality, is also a culture profoundly consumed by ego, and almost everyone in our society has their true identity confused with this illusory identity of "I."

It is not difficult to see how identification with the ego— and especially the feeling as though we need to protect, defend, enforce, and validate, the ego—can cause one to suffer deeply. We worry about things that threaten our reputation and our self-image as though they are actual threats to our health and wellbeing, simply because we have confused ourselves with our idea of ourselves.

The Buddha taught that the cause of suffering was ignorance—the ignorance of one's true nature that causes them to identify with the ego. He also noticed that the two most apparent qualities of the ego are craving and aversion.

Craving refers to our intense desires, the feeling that nothing is ever enough, and we are always in need of something else to make us feel complete, simply because we are not content with ourselves. Desires, in and of themselves, are not a cause of suffering, but it is our attachment to our desires which leads to our suffering. There is nothing wrong with wanting something, but if you want it so badly that you become miserable, irritated, anxious, impatient, and stressed, then the desire is unhealthy and will only cause you to suffer.

Aversion is also a desire—mainly our desire to feel safe and secure in our comfort zone. Once we have established a comfort zone, anything that causes us to step outside of it makes us suffer. We feel safe within our bubble of habits, beliefs, opinions, and what is known—and whatever is new, challenging, or unknown, is perceived as a threat to our bubble, and our biggest fear is that someday the comfortable bubble that we have created for ourselves will be popped.

A comfort zone is an illusionary boundary that prevents us from living life. Instead, we live in fear of the unknown and avoid anything that threatens the habits, beliefs, or concepts that make us feel safe. Life is uncertain, nothing can really be known, and by avoiding the unknown we only avoid life, and we ruin our experience simply by fearing that we will ruin our experience.

Avoiding pain causes pain, needing comfort makes us uncomfortable, the need for security produces insecurity. The ego, being made up of thoughts, concepts, and beliefs, can also be easily thought of, conceptualized, and believed by the thinking mind. In other words, the ego is something that the mind can know, and thus feel as if it has a sense of security with and control over. But Nature, as a whole, cannot be known by any means of conceptual knowledge, because it is far too vast to be understood by our linear way of perceiving, and this frightens the controlling mind, which feels as though it needs to understand life in order to feel safe and secure in life.

Thus, one who is identified with ego, feels much safer living in the world of their thoughts, beliefs, and concepts, and feels very frightened of the unknown. But the essence of reality is unknowable, and so the ego fears its source, which is why when we are confused with being the ego, we are afraid to look into our illusions, and afraid to discover our true selves, which cannot be understood by the same means of conceptualization.

When identified with the ego, one spends the majority of their time consumed by the thinking mind. They are rarely present with the reality of here and now, but are instead lost in the realm of their fantasies, ideas, worries, fears, hopes, regrets, and other mental constructs. They are not in touch with reality as it really exists, nor are they in touch with their hearts, their awareness, and the level of bodily feeling.

It is not difficult to realize the transparent nature of the ego. If we stop completely, not just outwardly, but inwardly, we will see that there is no truth to our self-image. Allow yourself to take a few moments to sit and observe the way that your mind behaves. You will notice that it is completely restless, thinking endlessly, jumping from one fantasy to the next, afraid of just relaxing into the peace of being without thinking, always resisting the silence of the unknown. If you continue to observe your mind, you might reach a state where the thoughts begin to subside, and you recognize them as clouds rising and falling in the sky of your pure awareness. You will notice that "I" along with all of the many thoughts attached to this "I" are nothing but illusions of the mind.

Being raised in a society, one must learn how to function in that society by learning to accept the language, laws, ethics, etiquette, codes, measurements, numbers, and above all roles. We have difficulty communicating with one another in society unless we can identify ourselves in terms of social roles—father, mother, son, daughter, boss, employee, teacher, student, artist, gentleman, lady, and so forth. This often causes us to confuse our identity with the many roles that we play, including the many stereotypes that are associated with these roles.

It is easy to see that we are not our roles, as a father or mother can just as easily be a teacher, an employee, an author, a church member, as well as a brother or sister. It is equally obvious to see that the sum total of these roles will still not be able to describe the true nature of the person themselves.

But the many things that form our sense of identity are vast, and some are more subtle, and less easy to recognize than our identification with our social roles. For example, who we consider to be "myself" is often made up of a history of selected memories and past events, which completely leave out the actual infinitude of events and experiences that actually occurred.

People cling to what has happened to them, or what they have accomplished, as a way to enforce their belief of who they are. Even if someone went through a very traumatic experience, they will refuse to let go of the memory of it because it contributes to their ego identity. As much as they would hate to admit it, many people find comfort in their suffering because it gives them an identity as a victim, and this enforces their belief in who they think they are. Indeed there are many delusional and psychotic things that we do in order to maintain our illusions.

But we are not our illusions, and our desire to cling to and maintain our illusions prevents us from realizing our true nature, and consequently prevents us from being at peace, being happy, and being free. Most people have invested so much time and energy into their illusions that the idea that they are not who they think they are is too frightening to even entertain. They would rather cling to their beliefs about who they are in order to stay in the comfort zone of their conditioning, and maintain their illusory sense of security.

Illusions can never give us an understanding of the Truth of life, and if we want to realize our true identity and be free of ego, we have to be willing to let go of our illusions, and understand that life cannot be explained by words, symbols, or social conventions. Ultimately, we must admit that reality cannot be known conceptually, and must be willing to transcend the world of conceptualization and measurement in order to see things as they really are.

The Answer Is YOU

14 Freedom

The whole aim of Hinduism, Buddhism, and numerous other philosophies is to attain a state of consciousness, which in Sanskrit is called *moksha* or "liberation." This state of liberation is the freedom that arises from discovering who we are when we are no longer identified with any role, thought, or conventional definition. It is the freedom that comes from realizing our original identity as Consciousness, the substance and source of all that is.

This form of self-knowledge is different from the typical way in which we view knowledge, as information perceivable by our mind and senses. Rather it is a form of knowledge that arises from knowing that one's true nature is ultimately unknowable, but nonetheless is inescapable, and undeniably who we are at our core. In the words of Shankara, *"For He is the Knower, and the Knower can know other things, but cannot make Himself the object of his own knowledge, in the same way that fire can burn other things, but cannot burn itself."*

This liberated state of consciousness is not something that can be an object of knowledge, rather it is a state of pure being that is beyond knowing, beyond duality, and beyond measurement of any kind. It is for this very reason that Indian philosophers speak so frequently of what *moksha* is not, saying very little, if anything, about what it is. Indian philosophy leads one to Truth by focusing on liberating the mind from all concepts of Truth, for concepts, no matter how elaborate or detailed they may be, can never amount to the real thing.

The practical way to liberation is a disentanglement of one's consciousness from every form of identification. This is where the process of self-inquiry, of *neti, neti* (not this, not this) comes in. This process leads one to the realization that I am not this body, not these sensations, not these feelings, not these thoughts, not these roles, not this personality, not the ego, not the idea of God or the Self. The ultimate reality of my life is not any conceivable object.

In the moment when every last identification of Consciousness with some object or concept has ceased, there comes forth from unknown depths a state of awareness which is absolutely free, a state of pure and absolute Being in which reality is experienced as whole, undivided, and inseparable from oneself. This state of nondual and undifferentiated consciousness is the state of liberation, or *moksha*.

Moksha is liberation from *maya*, liberation from the world of measurement in which we divide reality, and divide ourselves, into separate bits and pieces. It is not a state in which the sensory world of nature ceases to exist, as many who seek to attain liberation believe it to be. It is a state in which reality is experienced as nondual (*advaita*). God is not

One apart from the many, but is both the many and the One.

Moksha is liberation from the world of concepts, conventions, ideologies, opinions, beliefs, definitions, descriptions, labels, words, numbers, and symbols—all of which are created by the mind's measurement of reality, and are not reality itself. This world of measurement, or *maya*, is what so many of us are bound to, spending the majority of our lives in our heads and in our thoughts, rather than in our hearts and in this moment.

The person who is liberated from *maya* still experiences the world of form, still experiences reality, but he does not separate, measure, or divide reality in the same way that most people do. Rather he sees reality as one—not in the sense that all things have joined together as one, but in the sense that nothing was ever really divided, only thoughts of measurement divide reality, but reality is and has always been one undivided whole.

Measuring and dividing reality has its uses, such as when it comes to communicating an idea or message through language, but we so easily confuse the world as it is with the world as it is measured, described, and talked about—especially when we are taught from such a young age to classify and divide the world into these many names, concepts, and measurements.

The mind attempts to grasp the ever-changing reality of nature in its web of beliefs, labels, and concepts, which is why *maya* is usually equated with *nama-rupa* or "name and form." But it is impossible to actually grasp the world of form with names and concepts, and the forms that we try to grasp are also transitory, empty, and ever-changing.

This is why both Hindu and Buddhist philosophy proclaim the importance of realizing the impermanent and elusive nature of reality, and also point out that this realization is only depressing to a mind that tries to grasp at reality. But to the mind that lets go of this desire to grasp, and comfortably flows with change, the sense of impermanence and emptiness becomes a source of profound freedom and joy.

The fact that Consciousness or God is the underlying ground of reality is impossible to grasp as a concept, which is why the total elusiveness of the world is the teaching that lies at the root of Buddhist philosophy. Buddhism points out that one's true nature is unknowable—that one's identity, or ego, is merely a concept, and one's true nature is beyond conceptualization.

It was this realization of being unable to grasp or define oneself that led the Buddha to a state of perfect clarity and understanding—*anuttara samyak sambodhi*, or unexcelled, complete awakening—an experience of profound peace, clarity, and joy that is incapable of being described by words.

The fundamental difference of Hinduism and Buddhism is that Hinduism proclaims our true nature is the one Self of the universe—while Buddhism proclaims that in reality there is no-self. The Buddha did not actually imply that there is no real Self at the core of the universe, but rather that there is no Self, or basic reality, which can be grasped.

Freedom

He felt that the doctrine of the Upanishads that taught there was a Self was too easily misinterpreted, and easily became an object of belief, a goal to be reached, and a concept that the ego could cling to as just another sense of identity.

With this understanding, we can see that the true Self *is* no-self. Our true nature cannot be grasped, cannot be measured, cannot be confined or defined by a set of words, labels, concepts, or scriptures. To attain freedom, one must let go of the mind's desire to fit reality into mental labels and boxes—a habit that we have adopted from our cultural conditioning, and something we do in an attempt to enforce our ego and our illusory sense of identity.

The Buddha did not spend much time talking about the creation, origin, and meaning of the Universe. His focus was on providing people with a practical way to be free of their suffering. Though we can see from his teachings that he had profound wisdom and a deep understanding of the nature of reality.

He realized that there is an ultimate reality that is beyond beginning and ending, beyond up and down, beyond coming and going, beyond birth and death, beyond being and non-being—and he called this ultimate reality *Nirvana*. *Nirvana* is the absence of all notions, the absence of all concepts, and the absence of all mental constructions of any kind. It is not something that we run after or strive to attain; it is the very ground of our existence.

Many of us suffer because we are caught in the notions that we have a beginning and an ending, that we have a birth and a death, that we are the same or that we are different. But when we touch our true nature, the nature of *Nirvana*, we transcend all of these notions and become free.

These notions and concepts that our minds create are the source of all our fears, and consequently are the source of everything that prevents us from feeling love, freedom, and happiness. When we drop all of our notions and reach the state of *Nirvana*, we are no longer afraid of birth and death, of being and nonbeing, or of any of the ideas that our minds create.

True freedom is freedom from the known, freedom from concepts, freedom from the idea of being the one Self or of being a separate self. True freedom is the freedom of touching our true nature—the freedom to just be, right here and now, in the unknowable, indefinable, and immeasurable beauty and mystery of the present moment.

"At present your awareness is object knowing awareness. Unless you are mentally free from the objects you will not be free in the present moment. Don't think objects of you just physical, there are inner objects like ideas, beliefs, dogmas, desires, ambitions, craving to become some thing, fears, etc. If you can see the transiency of these objects your mind will be free from these objects and your awareness then becomes pure. Only pure awareness has the capacity to be present in the present moment because it has no distraction towards objects. The harsh reality is that your awareness is continuously distracted by the objects because you are investing some thing in them and so you will never be able to be present in the present moment. All the time you are projecting something from your past experiences which we call mind into the future thus missing the present. Missing the present means you are missing the life because life is always a new flow in the present moment and unless we are with that flow we will not be able to participate in life. At present what we call life is nothing but perpetuation of dead past and we cling to this past because we feel secure in the past because it is known and we are afraid to live life in the "present" which is always new and unknowable. We are all afraid of leaving the known which is like death and we don't dare to live the unknowable. To live with the unknowable we must first be free of inner and outer objects."

— *Suryanarayana Raju*

117

15 Presence

We typically view life as a collection of many different moments in time. We think that there is an immense history of previous events called the past, and an uncertain and unpredictable series of approaching events called the future, and in between these both lies a brief, fleeting, and ungraspable moment that we refer to as the present.

But in reality, past and future are merely concepts—concepts that exist in the eternal and ever-changing reality of the here and now. Everything is always happening now. When the events that we confine to "the past" were happening, they happened in this moment of now. When we think about the future, we are thinking about it in the moment of now. And when so-called future events do come, they will still be experienced in this moment of now.

The now is the only moment that ever exists. It is ever-moving, ever-flowing, and ever-changing, and if we try to experience it with the notion that there is a past and a future, it is indeed something that is fleeting, transient, and ever-fading. But when we realize that the now is all there is, and that no matter where our attention is focused, and no matter what happens it is always happening now, we learn to get out of the anxiety caused by our worries of the future, we learn to get out of our regrets and our misery caused by clinging to the past, and we relax into the freedom and peace that is available to us right here and now, in this very moment.

This state of directly experiencing reality without thinking about, or trying to define our experience, is a state that is commonly referred to as Presence. Freedom, or *moksha*, arises from being in this state of Presence. When we are here and now, we are in touch with reality, we are in touch with our body, in touch with our feelings, and are able to flow with and adapt to the changes that occur in our reality.

Presence is not something that you can think about, it is not something you can understand with the mind. To know Presence you have to be present. Thoughts are mental formations made up of words, labels, concepts, ideas, memories, images, and beliefs. But beyond these forms lies a state that cannot be named, described, or conceptualized. This is the state of Presence, the state of freedom from the world of *maya*, the world of name and form.

When consciousness frees itself from identification with mental forms, it becomes what we call enlightened, or pure consciousness. It is a state of nondual being in which we make no distinction between the experiencer and the experience, the thinker and the thought, or the knower and the known. There is not the witness on one hand and the reality being witnessed on the other. There is only this experience in which nothing is to be grasped as an object, and no one to grasp it as a subject.

Presence

This state of liberated consciousness is the state of Presence, and it is only in this state that we are truly free. When our attention is focused on being here and now, we do not feel fear, we do not feel stress or anxiety, we do not feel sadness, misery, or shame. We feel peace, we feel relaxed, we feel happiness, love, and joy. Presence is not something that can be thought of or understood with our minds; it is something that must be felt with our hearts.

The experience of Being, of living here and now, should be the primary focus of our lives, and the world of measurement, concepts, and notions, should be secondary, used only when necessary or of practical use. We should not spend our entire life experience living in the realm of our overthinking minds.

So many of us suffer because we are out of touch with reality in its suchness, out of touch with who we are at our core, and out of touch with the present moment in which all things are happening. If you are still struggling to grasp the meaning of what Presence is, it is because it cannot be grasped! You must get out of your mind and into this moment.

How do we get into the present moment? By trying to experience the present moment we only separate ourselves from it. We need to realize that we are already experiencing the present moment because the present moment is all there really is. With this realization, we can stop worrying about past or future moments, because they do not exist anywhere except as concepts in our minds.

When we focus intently on our experience now, nothing is left undone. We are fully present to share our attention and energy with whatever it is that we are experiencing, and are fully available to give our all to our experience. This is why the renowned Zen master Dogen described enlightenment as "*intimacy with all things*." When we are fully attentive to life here and now, we are free to allow what comes to come, and to allow what passes to pass. We do not have any fears, anxieties, or regrets when we live our lives with full awareness and Presence. Indeed the best way to take care of your future is to take care of life in the present moment.

To be in a state of Presence does not mean that you cannot plan for the future or reflect on the past, but you do not dwell on these thoughts, and are not attached to these thoughts because you understand that they are not reality as it is now. When you understand this, you will also find less need to think about the future, and less need to reflect on the past. Thoughts of both past and future only take us away from life as it exists now.

We are always in such a rush to get to the next place, next event, or next moment in time. We feel that the next moment is going to be better than the moment now, but because of this, we completely miss out on everything that is available to us right here and now. This addiction to impatiently rushing onward causes us to never really feel the joy of living, which is why so many people are full of regret on their deathbed, realizing that they rushed through their entire life, never taking the time to relax and smell the roses.

When we were young, most of us were placed in an educational institution that had a range of different grades that marked our progress. We were told that once we completed this schooling, we would be able to live life in society, and could follow our dreams and become who we wanted to be. We started out this journey of "becoming" in pre-school or kindergarten, and once we completed that we went on to first grade, then second grade, then third, fourth and fifth. Once we completed grade school we went on to middle school or junior high school, and then high school, and for some, college, and even graduate school.

Once finished with our schooling, we are finally able to go out into the world, into society where we get an occupation as a way to work toward this goal of becoming who we want to be. We work and work for money, status, and growth in our company. The years go by as we focus more and more on our future goals, and one day, when our goals are finally reached, we realize that we have spent the majority of our lives trying to achieve some level of success, of trying to become something that we were told we ought to become, and we realize that we missed out on so much of our lives because of this.

We spent so much time trying to become something, when what we really were looking for was not the feeling of becoming, but the feeling of Being. All we wanted was the freedom and peace that we were told would come from some time in the future, when really it was available to us in each moment of our lives.

Unfortunately, many people who experience the feeling that they missed out on their lives still do not realize that they have the opportunity to find peace and freedom in this present moment. Our society is so goal-oriented, so focused on accomplishing everything that we forget to just live and enjoy our experience of being alive.

"The meaning of life is just to be alive. It is so plain and so obvious and so simple. And yet, everybody rushes around in a great panic as if it were necessary to achieve something beyond themselves."

— Alan Watts

The universe isn't going anywhere. It has no destination, no place that it is to arrive at, it just is. So why must we rush so fast to accomplish, reach, or attain our desires? Why can we not just enjoy the beauty and magic of existence, of being alive in this unknowable and mysterious moment?

There is no need for us to struggle and suffer the way that we do. We do not have to take life so seriously. It is all just a play. We knew this when we were children, and we can realize it again now. The playful spirit of our inner child is dying to express itself, and our failure to let ourselves be is the reason that we suffer so deeply.

Presence

You are not a child anymore, and you do not have to worry about being traumatized or punished for being you. Sure there are people who might judge you, but you should not let what people think in their own minds determine the way that you feel in your heart.

The only people that will judge you for being you is the people that are too afraid to be themselves, and you shouldn't depend on another's opinion for your own sense of self-worth. Only the ego requires validation and acceptance to feel worthy, but you are not the ego, and it doesn't make a difference whether someone accepts you or not, what matters is that you give yourself permission to be your natural self, and to express yourself freely in the present moment.

Freedom comes from getting out of our fearful and restless conditioned mind, and entering into the flow of this moment—it comes from switching our thinking minds off, and engaging in the level of feeling and being, engaging in the dance of life as it is happening now. So much of our lives are spent living in the realm of our thoughts. We cling to our ideas and expectations about reality, when these are far from what reality actually is.

When we cling to our ideas, and our beliefs, we are trying to force our experience, and force ourselves to experience things in a certain way, rather than allowing our experience to unfold naturally. In trying to force our experience to be a certain way, we miss out on the experience that we were meant to have, and we do not learn the lessons or experience the joys that were available to us if we were to just let reality be reality, and let ourselves be ourselves.

We think that because we have invested so much of our lives in learning concepts, definitions, and beliefs about reality, that we actually know what reality is. But this is superficial knowledge. We see a tree and we label it as "tree" thinking we already know everything there is to know about it. But if we take the time to really sit with the tree and be present with it, we will discover infinite worlds of magic and life hidden within this beautiful expression of nature, things that weren't available to us when we confined the tree to the label and concept of "tree."

Our minds are so quick to label, define, and judge. We think that we know, but when we label or define anything, we only block ourselves off from discovering everything that it really is; we prevent ourselves from discovering the mysterious universe that exists just outside of our concepts and social conventions.

Reality is not something that can be grasped, and only the ego attempts to grasp it in order to be able to make it an object of knowledge that it can identify with. Presence, the state of pure Being, is a state that is free of all objects of knowledge, free of all concepts and grasping, and consequently, is also free of ego.

In order to experience the freedom and peace that comes from being in a state of Presence, one must be able to surrender their need to know, grasp, and understand reality, so that they may trust, let go, and allow reality to take its natural course. This is why so many religions and philosophies speak of surrendering oneself to God—surrendering one's idea of being a separate self, so that they may experience the love and the joy that comes from realizing one *is* God.

Surrender, used in this sense, does not refer to the act of giving up; it refers to the act of no longer resisting the present moment, but instead accepting it unconditionally. To surrender is to let go of how we think reality should be, and to embrace the way that reality is. This does not mean that we cease to take action or change a situation if it is undesirable. It means that we fully recognize our situation and act (or don't act) accordingly. To surrender to the present moment is to be wholly present and attentive to what is happening now, and not to be caught in or distracted by what might happen in the future, or what did happen in the past.

In order to surrender to the unknown, one must also have faith in the unknown. Many people confuse faith with belief, but the two are actually quite different. To have a belief is to have an idea of what reality is and to cling to that idea as being the ultimate truth. To have faith is to trust in the flow of nature, and to be open to the truth, whatever it may turn out to be.

When one has faith, one is able to trust that whatever course nature takes is always the most appropriate. With this sense of faith and trust, one is also able to relax and allow things to change in whatever way they will, without clinging to or being bound to this change. Our suffering arises from resisting reality, from resisting the moment and the course of nature because we desire for it to unfold in a particular way.

This resistance to nature creates a resistance within ourselves, and it prevents us from experiencing the joy and love of being in the present moment. When we are in a state of Presence we no longer resist reality or feel separate from reality. Instead, we feel a deep sense of belonging and connection to the whole of nature, a connection that can only be described as a feeling of unconditional love.

When we are able to surrender our ego and let go of our minds' clinging to conceptual understanding, we allow ourselves to be available to life as it exists in the present moment. When you tune into the here and now, you open yourself up to all that is, and infinite worlds become available to you. In Zen, the state of openness and Presence is often referred to as "beginner's mind"—a mind that does not know anything except for the fact that it knows nothing, and therefore leaves itself open to everything, which is why they often say that the true master is a beginner in every moment.

Presence

"One day I wiped out all of the notions in my mind. I gave up all desire. I discarded all the words with which I thought and stayed in quietude. I felt a little queer—as if I were being carried into something, or as if I were touching some power unknown to me...and Ztt! I entered. I lost the boundary of my physical body. I had my skin, of course, but I felt I was standing in the center of the cosmos. I spoke, but my words had lost their meaning. I saw people coming towards me, but all were the same man. All were myself! I had never known this world. I had believed that I was created, but now I must change my opinion: I was never created; I was the cosmos; no individual Mr. Sasaki existed.

—Sokei-an Sasaki

The Answer Is YOU

16 Love

Being in a state of Presence allows us to be free of our egos, and when we are free of ego, we feel our connection to the Universe, our connection to each other, and our oneness with the whole of nature. This feeling of connection is the indescribable sensation that many people refer to as Love.

The intelligent energy of the Universe, and therefore of our own being, is abundant, nurturing, and life supporting. The energy of the Universe is Love, and we are also Love. We emerge from this energy, live in this energy, and when we die we return to this energy. We are this loving energy, it expresses itself through us and as us, and no matter what we do or where we go we cannot ever separate ourselves from the Universal energy of Love. We can only feel separate from Love by resisting Love, and creating barriers within ourselves that restrict the energy of Love from flowing through us freely.

Love is merely a word that attempts to define this energy, as well as the sense of connection we feel when we are in touch with this energy—a feeling of appreciation, warmth, abundance, peace, acceptance, trust, and freedom that words are simply unable to convey. To describe what Love is, is almost easier to do by describing what it is not. Love is not fearful, clinging, or controlling. It does not criticize, judge, or condemn. It does not blame, ridicule, or make fun of. Love does not see others as being separate or unimportant. Love is not divisive, greedy, or selfish. It is not limiting or selective. It does not depend on circumstances or conditions. Love is not impatient, forceful, or expecting.

Love embraces all unconditionally. Love sees all as one. Love respects all as being a part of the one, and appreciates every part of the one by recognizing its impermanence and acknowledging its beauty as it exists now in this moment.

Many people fear love because it cannot be known conceptually, cannot be controlled physically, and can only be felt emotionally. But to the one who surrenders their fears, lets go of their ego's need to control, and embraces Love, they realize that Love is the source of true freedom, true bliss, and true purpose to the mystery of existence.

Do not seek anywhere but within for love. Do not build walls preventing love from entering, rather build an aura around you that is penetrable to allow a flow of love to constantly go through you. We are but a mere vessel of love. This vessel is connected to all things. Love is channeled through all these streams and is constantly flowing. If an attempt is made to contain this love, it will break the dam, thus causing an overwhelming amount of grief and sense of drowning. When love is allowed to flow naturally without trying to possess it, it gives one all that is needed. It protects you. It serves you. It guides you. And most of all it loves you. Love is meant to flow. Embrace the flow. It is always going through you. Do not ever doubt it. Love connects us all. The all is love itself, so that includes you. You are never without love. In fact, you ARE love."

— Jason Michael Ratliff

Our culture has a huge misconception of what Love is. We have tried to force Love, to find it in physical features, to look for it in sex and pleasure, or find it in what someone can do for us. Relationships are where most people look for Love, but relationships cannot give us love, they can only help us connect to the Love that is already within us. Failing to understand what Love is, we try to make it selective, and depend on the person that awakened the feeling of Love in us as if they were the source of our Love, and we suffer greatly because of this. Love is not something we can get; it is something that we are, something that exists within us, and all we need do is surrender to it, tap into it, and let it consume us wholly.

If we confuse love with attachment, with the need to feel safe, and the need to have someone we can depend on and fulfill our desires and expectations, we will only suffer, as we are not really acting in love, but in fear. Fear is controlling, dependent, and insecure, and stems from a lack of love, from a lack of realizing our true nature. Fear is not a quality of Love, it is a quality of ego.

If we can surrender our ego—surrender our need to feel

safe, our need to control, our need to fulfill our desires, our cravings, and our fantasies—we can dive into the unknown and allow Love to flow through us. Love does not make much sense to the fearful and conditioned mind, which is why the fearful ego creates barriers to prevent love from flowing freely through us.

But if we can break down these barriers that we have built within us, we can become channels of this unconditional love, and allow love to ripple outward from our being, impacting everyone and everything in the universe. Our mind defines reality to feel safe and comfortable with reality, but then we live in a conceptual box, and resist everything outside of the box, because we are afraid of the unknown.

But by being here now, by being in a state of Presence, we can embrace the unknown with Love. Whatever arises in our experience can be welcomed with Love, rather than being pushed away by fear. Everything we interact with can benefit from our loving Presence.

So many people suffer, just as we do. They may hide it well on the surface, they may be able to suppress their suffering, ignore it, or distract themselves from it—but deep within every human being lies an ocean of suffering, and our loving Presence can touch the suffering of others, and send them the Love, kindness, and positive energy that they so desperately long for.

Because of the present state of our culture, which operates under conditions of fear, violence, brutality, and other primitive qualities, every person that we meet is likely to have a range of traumas, negative conditioned habits, psychological issues, and other emotional wounds. By healing the psychological and emotional wounds within our own being, we are able to allow Love into our lives, and are able to share that Love with others, contributing to their own healing.

Simply by healing ourselves and allowing ourselves to be present, we can help heal the lives of those we come in contact with too. Healing ourselves is healing others, and healing others is healing ourselves. We are all one, and when we are in a state of Presence this becomes more than just an intellectual concept, but becomes an undeniable reality—it becomes our very state of Being. When you look another being in their eyes, and see beyond all of the differences and features apparent on the surface, you recognize their soul, you realize your connection to them, and you see them with the eyes of Love.

The mind is a powerful and beautiful instrument, but without Love, it becomes controlling, fearful, and mistrusting. The heart is also a powerful and beautiful instrument, but without wisdom it becomes illogical, unreasonable, and overwhelming. Wisdom without Love is dull and lifeless, and Love without wisdom is blind and irrational. If we can balance both the mind and the heart, both wisdom and Love, we can enter a state of coherence, a state of harmony, a state of stability—a state of Love with understanding.

In Buddhism, the two-fold nature of Enlightenment is referred to as a balance between wisdom and compassion. Buddhist monk and teacher Thich Nhat Hanh explained the necessity of this balance very well when he wrote: *"When you love someone, you want him to be happy. If he is not happy, there is no way you can be happy. Happiness is not an individual matter. True love requires deep understanding. In fact, love is another name for understanding. If you do not understand you cannot love properly. Without understanding, your love will only cause the other person to suffer."*

He goes on to explain an example of Love without understanding by relating it to his distaste for durians—a fruit local to Southeast Asia: *"If you were to say to me, 'I love you so much I would like you to eat some of this durian,' I would suffer. You love me, you want me to be happy, but you force me to eat durian. That is an example of love without understanding. Your intention is good, but you don't have the correct understanding."*

It is important that we have a balance of both Love and wisdom. The way we express our Love might not be compatible with someone who is not ready to receive such a powerful and encompassing sensation that one in a state of Love is willing to express. If we are truly present with others, we can be sensitive to their energy and the way that they feel, and we can interact with them on a level that resonates with their state of being. We can still express our Love, but some may be more receptive to our Love than others, and that is okay—we can meet others where they are on their journey.

Love

To be in a state of Presence allows one to be receptive to their environment, sensitive to their situation, and able to always react in a manner that is most appropriate. It is a beautiful thing to be in a state of Presence and to allow Love to flow freely through you, as you realize that Love is not dependent on any person, place, or thing, but merely on your ability to opening yourself up to the energy of Love that is already inherent within you.

When I was traveling in Peru, the Shaman that I was staying with called this state Heart-Centered Presence. When we get out of our minds and engage in this moment, we also engage into our hearts and our connection with all that is, and it is this state of Heart-Centered Presence that allows us to truly experience freedom and Love, and makes us capable of helping others feel freedom and Love as well.

When we are free from *maya* and the world of concepts and measurements, we experience reality openly with a state of loving awareness. This loving awareness does not judge, criticize, or condemn anything; it accepts, cherishes, and embraces everything. This loving awareness is not aggressive, selfish, or violent; it is gentle, selfless, and peaceful. When we are fully present in our loving awareness, we are no longer disconnected from reality, but deeply in touch with it. We no longer cling to our ideas and beliefs about reality, but experience it directly and flow with it. Presence is something that we feel and tap into, not something that we think of and describe.

When we are present with another person, it means that we are attentive to them and that we respect them in their essence. When they speak, we listen, and try to feel what it is they are communicating—we are not just waiting to reply so that we can state our opinion and enforce our views on them. Without Presence, true communication is not possible. When two people are present with each other, they allow an open channel of Love and connection to flow freely between them.

Human beings are naturally expressive, but out of fear people often hide their inner beauty and creativity. Every human being wants to express themselves fully, and if we can just sit with someone and give them our loving Presence, we give them the opportunity to be themselves, to express themselves, and allow themselves to be heard— which is really all that so many people long for. If we can open ourselves up to the dimension of here and now, Love, happiness, and freedom become our very nature.

To be in a state of loving Presence is to be in a state of awareness that is calm, relaxed, open, attentive, alert, genuine, caring, sincere, curious, and nurturing. It is a state in which we are so immersed in the dimension of here and now that we have no consciousness of self, no sense of separation from our environment, no fears or worries about the future, no regrets or grievances about the past. It is a state in which everything is perceived as new, as though we are experiencing it for the very first time—because we are, every moment the world is changing; nothing is really as we think it to be.

"You are a creature of Divine Love connected at all times to Source. Divine Love is when you see God in everyone and everything you encounter."

– Wayne Dyer

The Answer Is YOU

17 Resistance

Because of our identification with the ego, our lack of understanding our true nature, our social conditioning, and all of the traumatic experiences we have undergone in our past, we have built up many barriers that prevent us from allowing the flow of Love to enter our lives. Unless we look within ourselves, find these barriers, and heal them, we will not truly be able to open ourselves to the flow of Love that is ever present around and within us.

We create barriers within us to make us feel safe, and we almost always do this unconsciously as a reaction to something that has made us feel pain in the past. A perfect and very common example of this is when someone is hurt by a romantic partner, and makes a pact to themselves not to trust another person again. They allowed one traumatic experience to prevent them from giving anyone else a chance at being their partner.

This occurs so frequently because of our misconception of what Love is. We look for Love in other people, and depend on them for our feelings of Love, and when they are no longer able to provide us with these feelings, we become hurt and blame them for our suffering, when really we are at fault for giving so much of our power away to them in the first place. Love is something that exists within you, and you can only find Love within you.

The best kind of romantic relationship is when both partners have found Love within themselves, and then share that Love with each other, rather than depending on one another for their own feelings of Love. When we find Love within ourselves we can share our Love out of choice, out of joy, and out of a willingness to be happy and make others happy. If we look for Love in others, without having found Love within ourselves, we only cling to the object of our Love, depend on them, and constantly fear losing them— which produces a range of insecurities, fears, possessive qualities, and jealous tendencies that are so common in many relationships today.

Love isn't something that you get, something that you have, or something that you need to search for. It is something within yourself that you need to allow, something you need to trust, and something you need to open yourself up to. The only reason we suffer so deeply is because we do not allow Love into our lives, but instead resist it every opportunity we get.

The level of Love we do or do not feel is equal to the level of resistance we have within ourselves. Everything in the material world is constantly dying, constantly changing, and constantly being reborn. It is living and always new. When we try to cling to life, grasp it, or control it, we only restrict it, and we prevent ourselves from flowing freely with it.

Resistance

We have to learn to trust in the present moment, to welcome change, to allow life to flow in whatever direction that it wants. When we resist change or cling to expectations of how we think things should change, we only create our own suffering. We cannot stop life from living, we cannot prevent things from changing, and we shouldn't stress over what we cannot control.

Once we see that resisting life is ultimately futile, and that through our resistance we only cause ourselves to suffer, then we can choose not to suffer, and can choose to surrender to the present moment, and appreciate life as it exists in each moment.

Try to become aware of the resistance in your own life. Can you acknowledge when you are creating your own suffering? Can you see how your desires and expectations are what make you suffer? Can you see how your regrets, your clinging to memories, and your failure to let go of the past are also causing you to suffer? If we can be honest with ourselves, we will realize that the only time we suffer is when we resist the present moment—when we resist life as it exists right here and now.

It is never our situation that is the cause of our suffering, but our thoughts about our situation. The way we relate to life determines how we react to life, and the way we react to life determines how we feel about life.

If we want to be free, and if we want to allow ourselves to live in Love, then we have to be willing to stop resisting life, and to break down all of the barriers that we have built within ourselves that keep us imprisoned in our suffering. This often requires us to go to the places within ourselves that scare us, to look at the traumas that hurt us, to acknowledge why we created these barriers to protect us, and to realize that we do not need these barriers anymore. They have served their purpose and we can thank them for that, but we can let go of them, forgive the past, and forgive ourselves for causing so much of our own suffering because of our ignorance of who we are.

Enlightenment can only grow out of delusion, and if we hadn't suffered the way that we did, we would not be where we are now. But now we have decided that we do not want to suffer anymore, that we want to be free, that we want to heal our emotional and psychological wounds, and that we want to allow Love to flow freely in our lives.

Now that we have gotten this far on our journey, we can forgive the past and start anew. We can stop resisting the moment, we can stop clinging to our barriers for security as we realize they are really the cause of our insecurity, and we can find our peace, find our ground, find our stability, right here and now in the truth of our being.

Life may be unknown and uncertain, but this is what allows for it to be such a beautiful experience. If everything were already known it would take away all of the mystery, all of the excitement, and all of the adventure. The joy of life is in living. It is not a destination, but a journey. And when we learn to embrace life and all of its uncertainties with the openness and receptivity of our loving awareness, life becomes truly joyful, truly magical, and we become truly free.

"Your task is not to seek for love, but merely to seek and find all the barriers within yourself that you have built against it."

— Rumi, 13th Century Poet

The Answer Is YOU

18 Mindfulness

Getting out of our heads and into the present moment is not always as easy as we would like it to be. Actually, it is so easy that it can happen at any moment, but our minds have built up a great deal of resistance to the present moment, and it often takes some practice to create the habit of being here and now. The practice that enables us to do this is the practice of mindfulness.

Mindfulness is the energy of being aware and awake to the present moment. It is essentially a synonym for Presence, but it is also a practice that we can carry out in order to cultivate our Presence by being aware of our attention and what it is that we are focused on. Basically, mindfulness is the simple reminder to come back to the present moment whenever our attention becomes consumed by our thinking mind and our unnecessary mental self-talk.

When we notice that we are not here and now, but are lost in thought, we can stop our mind in its tracks and return our attention to the present moment. There are many ways in which we can effectively do this, but it is important to keep in mind that thoughts are not something that we suppress, condemn, or try to get rid of by force. As Carl Jung said, "*Whatever you resist persists*," and this as true for our thoughts as it is for anything else in our experience.

Rather than resisting thought, we should have a basic understanding of the limitation of thought, and understand deeply that thoughts are only symbols for reality, and are incapable of describing reality in its suchness. With this in mind, we can take thoughts less seriously, and not be so attached to whether we can follow a thought to its end.

It is also important to understand that thought is a product of the past, and cannot grasp the present moment. We only think in a language that is known to us—a language that consists of the information and concepts that we have learned from our culture. Therefore, thought is a product of conditioning and memory, and it carries with it a huge momentum of mental energy. Our thoughts will not immediately cease, but will gradually become less dominant and less apparent as this mental energy continues to lose its momentum.

Rather than trying to eliminate your thoughts or suppress your thoughts, practice developing a detachment from thought and understand that your thoughts are not who you are. Thoughts are not a bad thing, they can be very useful, and it is because of our ability to think critically that we humans have such an advantage over other living beings when it comes to our survival. The problem arises when the majority of our experience is dominated by thought, when we confuse ourselves with thought, and suffer deeply because of our thoughts.

A mind that forces out all thoughts and sensations becomes hard and rigid. As the Zen master Hui-neng said, a man with an empty consciousness is no better than "*a block of wood or a lump of stone.*" Rather than trying to make our mind empty and dull, we should try to make our mind like space.

Space contains all forms within it, but it is not bound to or affected by any of these forms. Space allows forms to appear, to be, and to disappear freely, remaining untouched as the essential background of everything. In the same way, we should not resist thoughts, but should allow all thoughts to come and go as they please, without attachment, remaining presently aware as the witnessing consciousness in the background of our minds.

The Sufi mystic and poet Rumi, explained it beautifully when he wrote:

"This being human is a guest house.
Every morning a new arrival.
A joy, a depression, a meanness,
some momentary awareness comes
as an unexpected visitor.

Welcome and entertain them all!
Even if they are a crowd of sorrows,
who violently sweep your house
empty of its furniture,
still, treat each guest honorably.

The Answer Is YOU

He may be clearing you out
for some new delight.

The dark thought, the shame, the malice.
meet them at the door laughing and invite them in.

Be grateful for whatever comes.
because each has been sent
as a guide from beyond."

When we are in a state of Presence and pure awareness, we welcome all experiences, allowing them to come and go freely. We do not push them away or try to grasp them, as this only creates a resistance within us, and prevents Love from flowing freely through us. When we are in this state of Presence we are open, and when we are open to life we have the freedom to live life to its fullest, without any fears, doubts, or uncertainties holding us back.

One of the simplest and most effective ways to come back to the present moment is to focus on your breath. By relaxing and consciously breathing, we unite mind and body, and our attention becomes focused on the here and now. Any time you are lost in your restless mind, try to remember to return your attention to your calm and natural breathing. You will find that this is a quick solution to taking a pause from the mind and reconnecting with your body and your awareness.

The body is always operating in the present moment— only the mind can get lost in thoughts of the past and future. However, when we fear thoughts of the future or think negatively of the past, this releases certain chemicals in our body that influence our health and well-being. This provides all the more reason why one should remember to stay calm, relaxed, and centered in the present moment.

Another way to accomplish this is by feeling into your body. If you take a moment to quiet your mind and tune into your body, you will notice that with little difficulty you can sense your body from within. Eckhart Tolle calls this your "inner body," and recommends that we always keep some part of our attention focused on the energy of our inner body, and by doing so, we will feel grounded in our Being, and will be far less likely to be overwhelmed or stressed by the circumstances of our outer environment.

We can also tune into the present moment by practicing gratitude. By acknowledging all of the things that we are grateful for in this moment, we become full of a sense of love, abundance, and contentment, and we realize that there is absolutely nothing that is lacking in this moment. A regular habit of being grateful can be a source of profound sensations of love, wealth, appreciation, joy, and fulfillment.

Doing something active that requires your concentration can also help you get out of your head and into the flow of the moment. While this practice, along with the other practices mentioned, can be seen as tools to help you be mindful of the present moment, the best practice for cultivating Presence is the practice of meditation.

19 Meditation

Meditation is a practice that has been revered for centuries by cultures around the world, and people have developed many different methods of meditation, but essentially it is a practice to help one be free of the mind and to cultivate a state of pure awareness. Unfortunately, many people today misunderstand the practice of meditation and the purpose that it serves. Meditation is not something that is done to attain *Nirvana*, to attain enlightenment, or to attain anything for that matter. As mentioned earlier, *Nirvana* is not something that can be attained; it is something that we already are. We only need to reconnect with our true nature and transcend all notions in order to experience Nirvana.

Therefore, meditation is not a practice in which we do anything. It is a practice in which we stop doing, in which we stop completely, both inwardly and outwardly, in order to reconnect with our source and realize the fundamental ground of our Being.

Meditation is the art of resting our minds and becoming aware. When we relax completely our thoughts start to dissipate, and we become aware of their transitory nature.

When we try to meditate to reach some goal, we only add onto the concepts and illusions that we are trying to see through. If we meditate as an attempt to get rid of our ego, it is only because the ego thinks it will be better because of it. The ego—the fearful and conditioned part of ourselves that clings to the thought of "I" for a sense of identity—so easily disguises itself by shifting its identification with a spiritual path. This is one of the ego traps that so many people easily fall into.

Many spiritual traditions bash the ego, and think that they have to resist the ego and fight it, but this only strengthens the ego. The more we try to transcend it, the stronger it becomes. Therefore, we should just let go of our effort to conquer and get rid of the illusion and just relax. When we relax into a state of Presence, the ego naturally dissolves in our loving awareness, without us having to do anything. It really is that simple.

In fact, it is because the truth is so simple that so many people have a difficulty in realizing it. The mind desires for an answer that is more complex, more technical, more conceptual—but this is only so it can know and understand it intellectually. All we need to do is stop this mental clinging to concepts and forms, and relax into the present moment.

Meditation is about resting completely—not just physically resting, but resting psychologically, letting go of all forms of mental effort. The mind never rests; it is always busy doing something. Mind has a very big job to do. It has to sustain the entire Universe. If our mind subsides, then there is no Universe. This alone should display clearly the illusory nature of the material world. There is nothing there when the mind stops maintaining this virtual reality.

Because of this, the mind feels that it has a big responsibility. It feels that it has to constantly perpetuate and construct the illusions of the material world. So to rest means to pause—to stop constructing the mental illusions. When you pause completely, the world of illusion ceases, and the true nature of reality is instantly realized.

Meditation is simply sitting just to sit, sitting just to be. It is nothing more than the act of resting, relaxing, and becoming aware. But the mind has a powerful momentum of mental energy, and it is not so easy for one to just completely stop forming the mental constructs, as they have become habitual.

Though with a little time, the habit energy of thought becomes less powerful, and the ability to rest in the present moment without thinking about it becomes more natural. To practice meditation, simply sit in a comfortable position, whether on the floor or in a chair, and focus on your breath. Do not follow the breath in and out of the lungs, just focus on the sensation of the breath as it enters and exits your nostrils.

Do not force yourself to breathe in a certain way, just allow your breath to flow naturally. As you do this, allow yourself to also just relax completely into the present moment—allow yourself to just be. In this state of calm and relaxed being, simply sit and observe the nature of your mind.

Center your gaze at the point between your eyebrows, and simply witness the way that your mind behaves, be the watcher of your mind that observes its reactions, its habitual patterns of thinking, and the many ways it continues to create thoughts and resist the silence of being in a state of pure awareness. A simple mantra for meditation is "relax and open," just focus on becoming aware—of thoughts, sensations, emotions, and whatever it may be that you experience.

Sit in this state for twenty minutes a day, or as long as it feels natural to you, and slowly the practice will become much easier as you learn to just relax and be still. It is extremely important not to feel rushed. Often we feel that we cannot sit still because we are anticipating what will happen next. Subconsciously, we think the next moment will be better than the current moment, and so we are always rushing through the moment in hopes of a better experience, failing to realize that it is really this hurried energy that is preventing us from being at peace. In meditation we do not have to do anything, we just have to stop doing—which is why our restless minds find it so difficult. But meditation provides us with a great opportunity to learn about our restless minds.

Meditation and mindfulness are both essentially practices to help us just relax with what is. We can always be in a state of total relaxation, and there is really nothing that has the power to take us out of this state of relaxation unless we give it that power. Even until the point of death we can be totally relaxed; in fact, we should be relaxed when we die as it is just as natural a phenomenon as living, eating, or breathing.

There are monks that practice meditating in an open jungle, practicing the art of total relaxation even while they are being eaten alive by mosquitos, gnats, and other insects. We do not have to put our bodies through such physical torment, but we can see that it is possible to relax in even the most stressful of circumstances. I am sure that the monks are also able to learn a lot about the fears and irritations that pop up in their mind, and are able to relax with those sensations and calm their worrying ego.

To what degree can you allow yourself to simply relax with what is—to relax with the sensations you feel, be it physical, emotional, or psychological? Whatever sensation you are feeling, pleasant or unpleasant, can you allow yourself to relax with it, and find peace and stability in the formless space of your awareness? If you cannot relax with what is, can you relax with not being able to relax? The degree to which we can relax in the present moment is not dependent on our circumstances, but on our minds, and on how we choose to react to our environment.

When I meditate, if I feel that I have an itch, or that my body feels it needs readjusting, I just sit with the feeling and try to relax with the sensation. Sometimes my mind will go crazy, thinking that it is going to die if it doesn't scratch that itch. But I know that the itch is not really a threat to my health, and so I practice to just relax with the sensation and learn about the agitation and discomfort in my mind.

I think that many of us also have psychological itches that we cannot help but scratch—desires, cravings, harmful habits, addictions, etc., and in meditation, if we just sit, relax, and observe these sensations, we can learn a lot about ourselves, and we can also learn that when we are grounded in our awareness we are safe, secure, and at peace—regardless of what is happening on the surface of our lives.

Eckhart Tolle describes mindful observation perfectly in his book, "The Power of Now" when he writes, *"Close your eyes and say to yourself: 'I wonder what my next thought is going to be.' Then become very alert and wait for the next thought. Be like a cat watching a mouse hole. What thought is going to come out of the mouse hole?"*

As we watch our mind with this intense and alert awareness, we notice that there is a gap between each thought, there is a space between the place where one thought ends and another begins. In this space there is no "I" there is no "me" there is no anxiety, no sadness, no fear or worry.

It is in this state that we come to realize our true nature. We realize that we are already enlightened. We are pure consciousness—perfect just as we are. When we realize this, we are perfect. When we don't realize this, we are also perfect. When we awaken to our true nature, there is no longer any desire to become something other than who we are. Every notion of who we are vanishes and along with it vanishes the fear, the suffering, the pain, the guilt, and the pride that is associated with our ego and self-image.

When we are ready to drop our previous perceptions of self, then enlightenment can happen at any moment. Just as the light of a single candle can illuminate centuries of darkness, the light of consciousness can illuminate decades of ignorance. Once our true nature is realized, we no longer live in the darkness of being a separate "I." We may still refer to ourselves as "I" when communicating through the social conventions of language, but we do not mistake this convention for who we are.

This realization has nothing to do with whether one has been meditating for many years or whether one has been studying under an impressive guru or teacher. It is simply dependent upon whether or not one is open to it—whether one is willing to let go of their identification with form, and realize the formless nature of reality.

A true spiritual path transcends all concepts and belief systems. It is not about becoming a Buddha, a guru, a saint, or even a better person; it is about deconstructing all of our mental illusions. As we begin to rest in the true nature of our awareness, we begin to see everything clearly. We see that the self has no basis or solidity—it is a complete mental fabrication. We also realize that everything we believe to be true about life is nothing but stories, fabricated around false identifications.

We have grown up to believe that we are our body, our thoughts, our personality, our likes and dislikes, our beliefs, our memories, our accomplishments, our race, our nationality, our social roles—but all of these are just stories that we tell ourselves. When we observe the illusory nature of these stories, they begin to dissolve in the ocean of our pure awareness.

This dissolution is not painful, as the illusions were never really real in the first place. Yet, people have a tremendous sense of fear and resistance when they believe that they are losing something. But life is constantly changing, and there is no permanent form that we can cling to and hold on to for a sense of security or identity. Nothing lasts, and eventually even this body will go.

In realizing this, we can see that our true identity is no-identity, and we can realize the preciousness of our existence as it is right here and now. True realization is realizing that everything is an illusion, everything is impermanent, ever-changing, ungraspable, and transitory. Without this realization there can be no freedom. Therefore, the goal of the spiritual path is to bring about this realization, not just to glimpse it once, or a few times, but to live in this realization in every moment.

Sometimes in meditation we have glimpses of the illusory nature of reality, but then we get up from our meditation practice and forget this insight as we continue to struggle and deal with everyday life. But when all of the layers of false identification have been stripped away, all that is left is pure consciousness. This is our original being, and it cannot be described by any of the forms that arise within it. Once our original being is fully realized we have true freedom, the freedom just to be alive without conflict, and to move with the present moment in whatever way that it flows.

"Meditation is offering your genuine presence to yourself in every moment."

— *Thich Nhat Hanh*

The Answer Is YOU

20   Reality Is a Mirror

Through meditation and mindfulness, we can learn a lot about ourselves and our conditioning—our mental habits, our neuroses, our attachments, our ego, our resistance, and the many illusions we cling to for a sense of identity. We can become aware of the habits that our ego has formed and we can discover within us where our resistance to the present moment lies.

As we become more aware of the layers of illusion within us, we can shed these layers so that they will no longer limit and restrict us from living freely. Just as you peel the layers of an onion to reach the core, we can peel back our layers of conditioning to realize that there is only consciousness at our core, and then there is nothing to restrict our freedom.

Perhaps the best way to learn about yourself is to see everything in your experience as a reflection of your state of being. This might be difficult to do at first, as often we are accustomed to viewing everything as separate from us, but with a little time you will begin to see yourself in everything, and you will see how both the positive and the negative aspects of your experience can teach you about something deep within yourself.

The Answer Is YOU

Take a look at your life and the circumstances that you are in. How much of where you are now has been determined by the thoughts you think and the actions you act out? The people in your life, the career that you have, the house you live in, the habits you do on a daily basis, etc.—how much of your reality has been created by you?

We attract people, things, and situations into our lives according to how we think, feel, and act. If there is something in your experience that you do not like, perhaps there is something in your mind or your lifestyle that you need to change.

Aside from what we attract into our lives, whatever happens to us in each moment will elicit some sort of reaction within us, and whatever that reaction may be, it can teach us about ourselves. If there is someone who irritates us, this person is triggering something within us to be irritated—they are bringing something within us to the surface that we can reflect on and learn from.

These habitual reactions are often called "triggers," and the best way to become aware of our conditioning is by realizing what our triggers are. If someone angers us, it is because we already have anger within us, and that person is only triggering this anger, and causing it to rise to the surface. If someone annoys us, it is often because we are seeing something in them that reminds us of something we do not like in ourselves. If someone makes us feel sad or inadequate, it is because we already carry these feelings within us, and they merely did something to cause these feelings to come to the surface.

"Everything that irritates us about others can lead us to an understanding of ourselves."

— Carl Jung, Psychologist

No one can really irritate us, annoy us, or make us miserable, unless they provoke these feelings that are already dormant within us. Can you recall a time when you felt that someone embarrassed you? Did they really embarrass you, or did you just allow yourself to feel embarrassed, and put the blame on them simply because they triggered a response that was already within you?

When we start to investigate emotions of embarrassment, fear, sadness, etc. and investigate where these feelings are, and who's thinking the thoughts or concepts that caused us to feel a certain way, we realize that it is none but ourselves who are thinking these thoughts. If you said something about me, and I felt embarrassed, then I embarrassed myself. And if I project out "you embarrassed me" then that is completely untrue.

If I think negatively about myself, and someone says something to me which I have said a thousand times to myself, and I lash out at them for saying something I have said in my head for years, then that is completely insane. If someone brings out an emotional response in me it is because there is a part of me that agrees with them on some level. If I want to cling to my delusions and defend my ego, then I will perceive that person as an enemy. If, however, I operate from the position of truth, and want to shed the layers of my ego and my conditioning, then I will realize that they are not my enemy, but my friend, because they assisted me in seeing and uncovering the next layer of illusion within myself.

Seeing things in this light is not always easy to do, and it requires that you take full ownership of yourself and your experience. The ego hates this of course, because it perceives itself as a victim, and perceives everything as some form of personal attack on "me."

If someone judges you, it is because they judge themselves. If someone acts out in anger toward you, it is because they carry this anger within them. If someone treats you with disrespect, it is because they do not respect themselves. The way we treat others is a reflection of how we treat ourselves. We can learn a lot about ourselves, and others, simply by observing the behaviors that we act out. However we act on the surface reflects something deeper within us.

If you start to see things in this way, and look at everything in your experience as a deeper reflection of yourself, you will come to some profound realizations about how you relate to yourself and how you relate to life. Many of us live in fear, and the biggest fear that most people have is the fear of judgment—the fear of what other people think.

Reality Is a Mirror

People lose themselves in the need to feel accepted by others. You don't need anyone to accept you, except you. Any time you worry that someone is going to judge you, that is really you judging yourself. You are the only one judging yourself. Anyone else that judges you is reflecting their own self-judgment and projecting it onto you. If you can realize this, you can let go of the heavy weight of self-judgment and fear that you have carried for so long, and you can forgive others for how they behave, because you realize that they are fighting their own internal battle.

When someone hurts us, we need to realize that it is because this person is hurting inside. They are only projecting their pain outward. What may appear as anger, abuse, or mistreatment on the surface, is really a deeper cry for help. This does not mean that they are justified in their actions, but it means that they are only human, and they suffer just like we do. Recognizing this, we can have true compassion for that person, and can see beyond their projected actions, and can give them our love.

By recognizing the truth that all words and actions reflect a deeper level of a person's state of being, we can see beyond the mere appearances of chaos, violence, and destruction, and can see the deeper level of suffering that lies at the root. By recognizing this, we develop compassion, patience, and love for others, as we can see a reflection of our own suffering within them.

To be free of our suffering, we must heal ourselves. And by healing ourselves, we become capable of healing others.

The true healer is the person who has healed themselves. The answer to freedom is within you always, as is the answer to Love. Whether you are trying to find peace, abundance, happiness, acceptance, liberation, or whatever it is that you seek—the answer is always YOU. The reality that you experience is a reflection of the deeper reality within your own being.

The amount of Love that we give and receive is a direct reflection of our present state of awareness. If we do not have Love within ourselves, we will not be able to give true Love to another, and will not be able to receive Love when it is offered to us. Indeed, we are only able to Love others as deeply as we Love ourselves. Much of the suffering in the world today arises from our failure to live in a state of Love, and our habit of living in a state of fear.

The state of the world now is merely a reflection of the collective human psyche. It is because we suffer internally that we project our suffering externally. World peace will only be possible in a world where people have found inner peace. If we have a world full of people with inner peace, we will have a peaceful world. Which is why the best way that we can heal the world is by healing ourselves.

The more that we heal our own conditioning, and break down the barriers that prevent us from living in a state of Love, the more we help others do so, too. Then the energy of Love is able to flow freely through us, without getting stuck on the blocks and barriers that we have built up. When we heal the resistance within us, we are capable of being fully present with others, and are able to give others our undivided attention. By resolving our own inner conflicts and personal issues, we become better able to assist others on their journey. By healing ourselves, we become available to help others heal; and by healing others we help ourselves heal.

The only reason that we require so much inner healing is because of the delusional culture that we live in and all of the traumas and conditioned behaviors that we have adopted from this culture. So by healing ourselves, we help heal humanity, as the things that require healing are the culture's delusions being expressed through us.

There is no separation between you and the world around you. The outer is but a reflection of the inner, and the inner is a reflection of the outer. The Universe is an extension of you, and you are an extension of the Universe. The best way to learn about yourself and your life is to see everyday life as your teacher. Do not look to books, to movies, to guides, to teachers, or to anyone other than yourself for answers that can only be found within you. Look to this moment, and whatever is arising in this moment. What can this moment teach you? If you look at your experience in the right light, everything and everyone becomes your teacher—everything becomes a mirror that can reflect a deeper aspect of yourself.

You do not need a guru, or a teacher, or anyone to point you to Truth. Be your own guru. Let life be your teacher. Look within yourself to find the Truth. Sure, there are times when we need a little help, when we need assistance and a little push to help us get back on the right path. But no one can tell you more about your own experience than you. No one knows your life and what is good for you better than YOU.

Life is our greatest teacher, and when we realize this deeply, we can see everything as a reminder to come back to ourselves. Then mindfulness and meditation cease to be practices that we do to be present, but become our very way of being. Everyday experience becomes a meditation when we live our lives with full Presence. You are the only one experiencing life from your perspective; no one can teach you more about yourself than the aspects of your own life experience.

"Nobody knows what is happening. Not Buddhists, not Christians, not government scientists. No one understands what is happening. So, forget ideologies. They betray. They limit. They lead astray. Just deal with the raw data and trust yourself. No one is smarter than you are. And what if they are? What good is their understanding doing you? Inform yourself. What does inform yourself mean? It means transcend and mistrust ideology. Go for direct experience. What do YOU think when YOU face the waterfall? What do YOU think when YOU have sex? What do YOU think when YOU take psilocybin? Everything else is unconfirmable rumor, useless, probably lies. So, liberate yourself from the illusion of culture. Take responsibility for what you think and what you do."

— *Terence McKenna*

---

21 Forgiveness

Once we become aware of our inner conflicts, our personal issues, the dramas and stories we make up for ourselves, our delusions, our conditioning, our negative habits, and harmful behaviors—we must learn how to heal them so that they no longer control our experience subconsciously. The most powerful method of healing our conditioning is to practice forgiveness.

Forgiveness is the tool that we can use to heal our traumas, to heal our conditioning, and to heal all of the negative aspects of our experience. When something triggers an emotional response in us, we can either behave in the way we have been habitually conditioned to behave, or we can acknowledge what has arisen within us and forgive it.

Forgiveness is a moment-to-moment practice in which we continually become aware of our personal issues and heal them with our love. We no longer push them away or sweep them under the rug. We embrace them, look into their cause, and let go of them.

It is not easy to admit that you have been living a lie your entire life, that you have confused your identity with an illusion, and have been clinging to your ego for a sense of identity. When we are heavily identified with the ego, the ego will do anything to defend itself and reinforce the notion that it is real and important.

Even if we can acknowledge the ego within us, and are ready to let go of its control over us, to actually surrender what we have held onto for so long, is not always an easy task. But when we see everything through the eyes of love, we can embrace the ego, love the ego, and forgive the ego.

By trying to fight the ego, resist it, or push it away, we only strengthen it. But by giving it our Love, we are actually giving ourselves the love that we have always longed to receive. The ego is simply the shadow of our own being, and when we have the courage and will, we can meet our shadow for the first time, and we can give it our Love. Then, just like a spotlight illuminates a dark room, our awareness shines on our shadow and replaces it with love and Presence.

The ego is always looking out for our best interests, even if it does not know what is really best for us. It just wants to ensure our survival. The ego should not be hated, condemned, and destroyed. It should be loved, thanked, and appreciated. When you give your ego this energy, it is replaced with Love.

When we put up barriers within ourselves, we do so because we think it is what is best for us. When the ego causes us to cling to these barriers for safety, it is only doing what we have trained it to do. We should not get mad at it or blame it for our suffering. We should acknowledge the ego when it arises, thank it for looking out for us, and then heal it with our loving Presence.

There are many parts of our being that we have been resisting, and they will continue to arise as we look deeper and deeper within ourselves. The deeper we look, the more layers of conditioning, trauma, habits, beliefs, attachments, and other negative aspects we will find. When these parts of us do arise, all we need to do to heal them is accept them, forgive them, and give them our love.

We do not heal our shadow by judging it, condemning it, or being ashamed of it. We heal it by bringing it into the light—into our love and our awareness. We heal it by looking into it, acknowledging it, feeling it, forgiving it, and making peace with it. Using our loving awareness, we can calmly look into our emotional wounds and begin to heal them. Until we make peace with the things that scarred us in our past—the things that made us judgmental, bitter, cynical, anxious, shy, depressed, or fearful—they will always play a role in unconsciously influencing our lives.

Until we make peace with our past, we will not be able to be at peace in the present. Allow yourself to touch your suffering, to look deeply into the parts of yourself that you have been resisting, so that you may heal these aspects of your being, and be free of them. Forgive yourself for ever harming anyone, whether you did so knowingly or unknowingly. Forgive others for ever harming you, whether they did so knowingly or unknowingly. Forgive yourself for all of the ways that you have treated yourself, doubted yourself, or done something you weren't proud of. Forgive yourself for looking for love in others, and forgetting to give it to yourself. Forgive yourself for creating all of the barriers within yourself that have prevented you from being you. Forgive yourself for losing yourself by trying to fit in to society, and give yourself the love that you have for so long looked for in others. Allow yourself to let go of your attachment to the thoughts and memories that are preventing you from being at peace.

Forgiveness is only possible where there is acceptance. Forgiveness is letting go of the past and accepting reality as it is now. And acceptance is the bridge between you and a life of true freedom. Accept the pain that you have experienced in your past, accept the wounds, accept the traumas, accept your conditioning, accept yourself! Once you have forgiven the past, and have made peace with the past, you no longer have anything holding you back from being at peace now in the present moment. And once you have gotten to the point where you are truly capable of accepting each moment, and are able to accept yourself in each moment, you have reached a level of freedom that no one can take away from you.

22 The Path

The path to self-realization is a pathless path. No matter where you go or what you do, YOU are always there. You only need to let go of the barriers that prevent you from being you, so that your true and unknowable nature can express itself through you freely. We are all instruments of divine Love, and our conditioning has made us go out of tune. Heal your emotional wounds so that you can allow the music of your soul to play its magical symphonies without resistance, without fear, and without any limiting barriers.

There is no path that can lead you to yourself, as you are always YOU. In the words of Lin-chi, *"If a man seeks the Buddha, that man loses the Buddha."* You already are that which you seek. You cannot reach enlightenment, or reach *Nirvana*, all you can do is realize that you already are enlightened, *Nirvana* is your natural state—you just need to remove all of the resistance within yourself that is preventing you from living in this enlightened state.

While there is no path that can lead you to yourself, there is a path that can help you remove the causes of suffering in your life, and can help you live a way of life that is in harmony with your true nature, in harmony with the environment of which you are an intricate part, and in harmony with other living beings and life as a whole.

This path is known as "The Eightfold Path," and it is the path that the Buddha developed to help people be free of their suffering. Keep in mind that everyone's circumstances are different, and therefore no one is on the exact same path in life. There is no one path that you should follow; you should follow your intuition, as it knows how to guide you best through your own direct experience. The Eightfold Path is merely an outline for how one can prevent causing their own suffering—it is by no means a path that you must strictly adhere to—it is just a practice that you can take what you need from, and leave what you do not need.

The Eightfold Path is the last of the Four Noble Truths, and to understand the path, one should have an understanding of the Four Noble Truths. The Four Noble Truths are patterned on the traditional Vedic form of a physician's diagnosis and prescription: the identification of the disease, and of its cause, the pronouncement as to whether it may be cured, and the prescription for the remedy.

In the case of the Four Noble Truths, the disease is our suffering. Therefore, the Four Noble Truths are: suffering exists, there is a cause to suffering, there is a way to be free of suffering, and the Eightfold Path is the remedy that can cure us of our suffering.

The Path

The first Noble Truth is that suffering (or *dukkha* in Sanskrit) exists. Everyone suffers to some extent. The first step in healing our suffering is to recognize our suffering. The Buddha said that to suffer and not know that one is suffering is more painful than the burden endured by a mule carrying an unimaginably heavy load. We must first recognize our suffering before we can work on being free of it.

The second Noble Truth is the origin, cause, roots, nature, or arising of suffering. After we recognize our suffering, we need to look deeply into how it came to be. We need to acknowledge the spiritual, mental, emotional, and material foods that we have ingested that are causing us to suffer.

The third Noble Truth is the cessation of creating suffering by refraining from doing things that make us suffer. It is true that suffering exists, but so does joy and happiness, and we can determine whether we experience suffering or joy by thinking and acting in a way that is conducive to how we wish to feel.

The fourth Noble Truth is the path that leads to refraining from doing the things that cause us to suffer. This is the Eightfold Path, or "The Path of Eight Right Practices" in Chinese: Right View, Right Thinking, Right Speech, Right Action, Right Livelihood, Right Diligence, Right Mindfulness, and Right Concentration.

The Eightfold Path has also been called "*arya ashtangika marga*" or "a noble path of eight limbs," which points to the interconnected nature of these eight elements of the path. When you correctly practice one of these elements, you are practicing all eight of them. Each one of the practices points you to a state of being that is of true Presence, true understanding, true purity, and true freedom. Please use your intelligence to apply these practices in your own daily life as you see fit.

Right View

Right view is first of all a deep understanding of the Four Noble Truths—to realize that while we may suffer, there are people who have become free of their suffering and it is possible for us to become free too. Right view is the ability to determine what contributes to our suffering, and what contributes to our healing—what is wholesome and what is unwholesome.

Viewing our minds once again as a garden, we can see that within us we carry both wholesome and unwholesome seeds. If you are a happy person, it is because the seed of happiness is within you. But the seed of sadness is also within you. Which seed will flourish in the garden of our mind is determined by which seed we water with our thoughts, feelings, and actions.

Through mindfulness, we can become aware of the seeds within us, and consciously choose to water the seeds that we want to flourish. Things take time to heal, and it will often require repetitive watering of the wholesome seeds within us before they outgrow the unwholesome seeds that we have watered in our past.

When a flower is dying, you do not blame the flower—you look to the soil, the minerals, the water, the air, and the sun. When we recognize our suffering, we do not need to blame ourselves, we just need to look at all of the things that have contributed to our suffering, and stop indulging in the things that contribute to it, and begin indulging in the things that will contribute to our joy and our freedom.

When one person approaches us, we might feel tense or anxious. But when a different person approaches us, we might feel relaxed and peaceful. In this way, we can see the seeds that are in us, the seeds of fear and anxiety, and the seeds of relaxation and peace. When we acknowledge the seeds, when we acknowledge the habitual reactions within us, we can choose whether we want to continue to act out of habit, or whether we want to act in a way that is more wholesome, a way that will not water the seeds of fear in us, but will instead water the seeds of Love.

The seed of awakening is also within us. Awakening is to wake up and realize the way that things are. We can water this seed by becoming aware of the illusions in our lives—the stories we tell ourselves, the beliefs that we cling to, the judgment in our mind, our negative habits, and all of the egoic behaviors we have adopted—and by refraining from watering these seeds, refraining from continuing to live in a world of illusion and deception, but instead choosing to see things as they are, and live in a world of peace and awareness.

To water the seed of awakening in us, we need to understand that the way we experience reality is a result of our perception, and as the Buddha once said, *"Where there is perception, there is deception."* Most of our suffering comes from our wrong perceptions. We have adopted certain views, beliefs, and understandings about reality that simply are not true, and we see through the lens of our false perceptions, creating our own suffering because of it.

To see things clearly, as they are, is to have Right View. This means that we perceive things openly, without instantaneously labeling them, judging them, and defining them with our minds like we so often do. To be in a state of Presence, a state of open-mindedness, a state of sincere awareness, and a state of curious understanding, is to have Right View, and when we have Right View we are able to distinguish what is true from what is illusion, and we are no longer fooled by illusions but are able to live our lives centered in Truth.

Sri Nisargadatta Maharaj once said that, *"the other world is this world rightly seen."* We can open ourselves up to a new world when we view this world in the right light. When we have Right View, we do not cling to our ideas, our notions, and our thoughts, we let go of the need to define reality and experience reality openly, we see reality as it is in this moment, and allow it to flow without clinging to reality and resisting this flow. To have Right View is to be an open channel in which your genuine Presence is free to naturally express itself.

When we have Right View, there are no wrong views, because in truth, all views are wrong views. No view can ever be the truth. It is just from one point; which is why it is called a point of view. If we view things from a different point, we have a different point of view, and realize our first view was not entirely correct. To have Right View is not to collect certain views about reality, but to eliminate all wrong views. Right View is the absence of all views.

When we water the seed of Right View in us, we water the seeds of every other practice on the Eightfold Path. Right Thinking, Right Speech, Right Action, Right Livelihood, Right Diligence, Right Mindfulness, and Right Concentration can only be possible when we have Right View. Likewise, when we practice any one of these Eight elements of the path, Right View arises out of it. Right View is both a cause and an effect of all of the other elements on the path.

Right Thinking

Once we have established Right View within us, we also have Right Thinking, and if we train ourselves in Right Thinking, our Right View will improve. Thinking is the speech of our mind, and when we think thoughts that are wholesome and clear, our speech and our actions will become wholesome and clear as well.

To have Right Thinking is to reflect how things are, not to perceive them in an illusory way or a way that will strengthen our ego. When we have Right Thinking, we do not make assumptions, or jump to conclusions that may not be true. When we have Right Thinking, we are present with things as they are, which also means that we do not allow our thinking to take us away from the reality of the present moment.

Our mind is often thinking one thing while our body is doing another, but when we practice mindfulness, our mind and body are unified, and our thoughts become less apparent, less frequent, and less controlling, as we see clearly that they are less necessary than our mind believes them to be. When we do think, our thoughts are clear, and we do not get mixed up in our thoughts or cling to thoughts that distract us from what we are doing here and now.

Much of our thinking is unnecessary, and these unnecessary thoughts only limit and prevent us from experiencing the freedom that we can experience when we allow ourselves to be here and now. It is like we have a cassette player in our head—always running, day and night—and this constant stream of thoughts creates anxiety, stress, and fear within us.

When we recognize that our minds are caught in this loop of thinking we can ask ourselves, "What am I doing?" By doing this we can bring our attention back to the moment and can give our Presence to whatever it is that we are experiencing. The mind is always in a rush, and it always wants to complete things quickly, but when we rush through life we miss out on life, and we also do not give ourselves fully to the moment through which we are rushing. When we stop to take our time and give our Presence and Love to what we are experiencing, even things like doing the laundry, or taking out the garbage, can become peaceful and blissful experiences.

When we recognize that we are making assumptions, or are worrying about the future outcome of something, we can stop our mind in its tracks and ask, "Am I sure?" Our wrong perceptions can quickly cause us to panic and suffer, but if we can refrain from making assumptions, we can focus our attention on what is true, what is necessary, and what is beneficial to our well-being and the well-being of others.

Humans are creatures of habit, and the thoughts we think and behaviors we act out are also habitual in nature. We think the way we do because it is how we have conditioned ourselves to think. We act the way we do because it is how we have conditioned ourselves to act. When we realize that our habits have been created by ignorance and illusion, we can consciously replace them with wisdom and truth. And like any habit, the more that we practice it, the stronger it becomes.

When you notice a negative habit or negative pattern of thinking, just recognize it, smile to it, and replace it with your Love and awareness. Engrain a new pattern in your brain, a pattern that will contribute to your peace, and not your suffering.

When we have this attitude toward the unwholesome aspects of our experience, we are able to transform them into wholesome aspects. This is a form of mental alchemy. Alchemy is the art of transmutation, and the most powerful alchemy that we can perform is the transmutation of fear to Love, ignorance to wisdom, and illusion to Truth.

To live in this state of loving awareness, in which we embrace the dark with our light, is to have the "mind of love" which Buddhists refer to as *"Bodhichitta"* or "enlightened-mind." To have *Bodhichitta* is to be motivated by great compassion for all sentient beings, which becomes truly possible when we release attachment to the illusion of existing as a separate self.

By cultivating understanding within ourselves, we can bring happiness to many others. It is the realization that we are not separate from one another that produces the desire to be of service to others, and this desire is what motivates us to become free of our illusions and to practice mindful living.

When *Bodhichitta* is at the foundation of our thinking, everything that we do or say will help others to be free. To be free of our suffering, and to help others be free of their suffering, we must recognize the unwholesome qualities within our being, and transform them into positive qualities.

When we have a flat tire, our vehicle cannot move properly. In order for our vehicle to run smoothly again, we have to change the flat tire and replace it with a new and functioning tire. Likewise, when we have a negative pattern of thinking, our body cannot act properly. In order for us to act properly, we need to replace the unwholesome and negative pattern of thinking with a new pattern of thinking, one that will help us function better.

Right Thinking is thinking in accord with Right View. It is a map that can help us find our way, but once we find our way, we must learn to put the map down and fully embrace our experience. When you practice Right View and Right Thinking, you dwell deeply in the present moment, and are in touch with what is. Then you are able to see things clearly, and are able to water the seeds of peace, joy, love, transformation, and freedom.

Right Speech

Not many of us are aware of just how powerful our words are. Words are energy, and the power of speech is able to create worlds, liberate minds, or destroy lives. When we are aware, we can use our speech to help rather than harm the lives of those we interact with. Our society would likely collapse without the use of words or language. Words allow us to communicate to each other messages from within.

With words, we can compliment someone and let them know how beautiful they are, how special they are, and how valuable they are. We can also put them down, make fun of them, and tell them that they are worthless. Whether we want to use our speech for Love, or for violence, is up to us, but regardless, every word that we speak has tremendous power.

Some even suggest that is where the word "spelling" originates, as though with every word we speak we are casting a spell to create the type of world we want to live in. Words have that much power. Even the words that we say to ourselves are powerful, which is why Right Thinking is so important.

How many times have you suffered in your past, simply because of the words that someone said to you? How many times do you think you have knowingly or unknowingly caused someone else to suffer because of the words that you said to them? We fail to acknowledge just how much power our words carry.

Adolf Hitler was able to lead an entire nation into ignorance, and kill millions of innocent people, simply by using the power of his words. People are hurt, violence is spread, wars are started, and nations are destroyed, simply through the destructive power of words.

Words also have the power to heal, to spread Love and kindness, and to help people become free of their suffering if we use them in a wholesome way. So many people use their words for violence, and will even speak negatively to another they love as long as it allows them to get their point across. But what is more important: being right or being kind? Does it matter if you get your point across if the other person is suffering because of it?

We need to recognize the power that our words have, and vow to use our words for healing, not for harming. Right Speech is based on our Right Thinking, as speech is our thinking expressed aloud. When we speak to another, we allow them to hear the contents of our mind. Our speech is a reflection of our mind, and when we think loving thoughts, we express love through our words.

We can become more aware of the subtle nature of our thoughts and our conditioning by noticing the way that we speak to others. How do you act in conversation? How do you speak about yourself? How can the words that you speak be seen as a reflection of the contents of your mind? Often when in conversation we speak from how we have conditioned ourselves to talk. We speak half-truths, we speak in slang, we speak in ways that we think will allow us to be perceived as "normal." Observe the way that you speak in conversation—you will learn a lot about your mind and your conditioning.

To practice Right Speech, we must also develop the skill of deep listening. If we cannot listen mindfully, we cannot practice Right Speech. No matter what we say to another will not be mindful, because we will only be speaking our own ideas, and will not be speaking in response to the other person.

Many people have a habit of not listening to what the other person has to say, but rather wait for an opportunity to state their opinion. When two people who have this habit have a conversation, it is not a real conversation, but a battle of two egos trying to reinforce their illusions.

Most communication is non-verbal, and has to do with our body language, our facial expressions, and the energy of our state of being. Deep listening allows us to tune in to what is beneath the surface, and see what someone is really communicating, beyond just the words that are coming out of their mouth.

When we are able to listen to another person with full Presence, we can respond accordingly. But without that ability to listen, Right Speech is not possible. So many relationships have failed because of the partners' inability to listen to each other. So many people are frustrated because they go unheard, with their feelings unacknowledged. Often, all people really want is just for someone to be present with them and listen to what they have to say, and if we love someone, the least we can offer them is a set of open ears for them to express themselves.

When we listen fully, we are in a state of Presence, and the more we strengthen our ability to listen, the more we enable ourselves to live in a state of Presence. Try to close your eyes, relax, and just listen to your environment. Listen to all of the sounds around you, notice the deeper silence that all of these sounds are arising from, existing in, and returning to. By cultivating the art of listening, we cultivate our Presence, and are able to become free of our minds and the endless self-talk that accompanies a conditioned mind.

Just as important as the ability to speak is the ability to be silent. And often Right Speech consists of remaining silent, and not saying harmful words or engaging in a conversation in which harmful words are being spoken.

Our speech is a reflection of our minds, and if we want to live in Truth, we should only speak in accordance with the Truth. I remember reading a passage that asked, "*Imagine if every word that you spoke was tattooed on your skin, would you be more careful with the words that you spoke?"* That is a powerful question to ask ourselves.

The words that we speak play a major role in determining the reality that we experience. If we want to experience a loving reality, we should learn to view things from a position of love, to think loving thoughts, and to speak words of love, beauty, and kindness. Imagine that every time you speak a word you are speaking your reality into existence. What kind of words would you say? What kind of reality to do you want to live in?

Right Action

Right Action is the Right Action of the body—it is the practice of acting in accord with our Right View, Right Thinking, and Right Speech. Right Action is to practice nonviolence toward oneself and others, to act in a way that promotes, health, love, and happiness, and prevents, illness, harm, and suffering.

It is not difficult to recognize the power that our actions have, but many of us are unaware of our actions, and we cause unnecessary harm because we act out of ignorance. Our actions affect more than just our immediate surroundings. Every single one of our actions reverberates throughout the cosmos for eternity. Whether we choose to act out of love or fear affects more than just us. We are responsible for the energy that we put out into the Universe.

One of the best examples of this can be found in the current harm that modern industries are inflicting upon the planet. These harmful industries are a reflection of our collective actions. We see the damage that many of these industries cause, and we feel that we are powerless to stop them. Yet, we continue to contribute to them every day by supporting them with the money that we spend.

We think that it is harmless because we are only one small portion of the people contributing, and so we put the blame on society at large. But if every individual is blaming society at large, we are all really just escaping taking responsibility for our own actions.

This kind of collective blame makes us feel less responsible for our individual actions. But we are all responsible for the state of society.

Society is made up of individuals. If we want to heal society, we need to heal ourselves. If we want to stop destroying the planet, we need to become aware of our actions and stop contributing to the industries that practice unsustainable methods of production.

I can relate an example of collective blame to my own experience, but on a much smaller scale. When I was in Peru studying to obtain a certification in Permaculture Design, the community I was staying with was off the grid, tucked away in a mountain valley far from the luxuries of modern civilization. This was beautiful, but also very challenging for the many people who had not spent such a long period of time in a remote location.

The meals were served in giant pots, and one by one we all lined up to get our portions of the collective meal. Because there were so many people in the community, and the amount of food was limited, some individuals developed a mindset of scarcity, and began to take more than their fair share.

Because of this, the people at the back of the line would end up with less than everyone else. They had to suffer because of the fearful actions of others. This community was full of loving individuals, but because of the given circumstances, some individuals allowed the mindset of fear to get the better of them.

If everyone had taken their fair portions, there would have been plenty of food to go around. But because of the limited amount of food, they took more than they needed out of fear. When this was brought to the attention of the community, nobody felt that they were responsible for the lack of food, because each person that took more than their fair share thought they were only taking a small amount extra, and that they couldn't possibly be at fault for the situation at large.

They failed to realize the effect that their individual actions had, and did not realize that they were contributing to the problem. This is a very minor example of how collective blame can make us feel less responsible for our actions, but I think it is a good one to get the point across.

What we do as individuals either contributes to or detracts from the community at large. If we support industries that harm our planet, essentially we are the ones harming the planet. Many of us are not aware of exactly what these industries are doing, as they operate out of sight from our everyday experience, and we only come into contact with the finished product.

It requires a little bit more awareness on our part to look into the companies that we are supporting, but we can also use our intelligence to think of what might be involved in the process of production based on what makes up the finished product.

By looking at the labels on our food, for example, we can see whether something we purchase is organic, or conventionally grown (with pesticides). If it is conventional, and we purchase it, we are contributing to that industry and strengthening the demand for that market. Which means that, in this case, we are supporting the destruction of our soils, the destruction of habitats and ecosystems that depend on healthy soil life, the pollution of the oceans, the pollution of the air, and even physical harm to our own bodies.

According to the Stockholm Convention on Persistent Organic Pollutants, 9 out of the 12 most dangerous and persistent chemicals are pesticides used in conventional agriculture. These chemicals are not only hazardous to our health, but they are a huge threat to other living beings, and to the planet as a whole, and if we continue to support this industry, we are only contributing to our own destruction.

When chemicals that are designed to kill are introduced into delicately balanced ecosystems, they can set damage in motion that reverberates through the food web for years.

Pesticides contaminate the insects that are in direct contact with them, and they also contaminate the animals that eat those insects.

Even bees—which pollinate a majority of our food, and which we depend on for our food—are endangered because of the use of agricultural pesticides. Aside from pesticides, there are many other industries that we contribute to without realizing the harm they are causing to the planet at large.

The animal agriculture industry, for example, is the biggest threat to the environment, as there are nearly 80,000,000,000 (eighty billion) animals killed each year for food. To provide food for these animals, mass amounts of land are cleared, killing even more life and all of the ecosystems that depend on that life for their survival. Nearly half of the Earth's land is used for livestock purposes. We use up far more resources sustaining livestock than we do sustaining our own species.

To the individual person purchasing a solitary item at the grocery store, they may not feel like they are affecting much. But if we were to see the entire process of how that product got to the grocery store where we purchased it, we would think twice before buying it. The products that we buy determine the markets that are popular. When there is a demand, companies will continue to create a supply, otherwise they would go out of business. If everybody boycotted a certain company at once, that company would be bankrupt within a matter of weeks. Corporations depend on consumers. When we demand healthy products that are sustainably produced, we will create that market, and companies will have to meet the demand.

We need to realize that the consumers determine the markets—we decide which industries we want to support. This is a very powerful thing to realize. Imagine just how much positive change could be made when an entire society was consciously aware of the effects of their actions. It is not an unrealistic thing to imagine, and this can become our collective reality—but only once we make it our individual reality. We have to take responsibility for our own actions and the effect that they have on the world. We are all interconnected to one another, and even the smallest actions affect the Universe as a whole.

The small actions we take each day create habits of behavior, and our habits of behavior determine the lives that we live. If we can be aware of the small actions we perform, and can choose to act with love, we habitually train our behavior to reflect our loving awareness.

The importance of living a life that does not condone violence is immense. Our culture glorifies violence through different forms of media, and pollutes the minds of those who are exposed to these toxic forms of media. Because of this, we have become desensitized to violence, and are not as disturbed by violent acts as we should be. Violence is not something that should be glorified. Nobody wants to experience pain; no one wants to suffer. Whether they are a human, an animal, a plant, a mineral, a cell, etc.—all living things want to live. The only living things that do not want to live are humans that suffer deeply because of their wrong perceptions. But when we heal our perceptions, heal our ignorance, heal our conditioning, and see things clearly, we see that suffering is a reality for so many people, and we have the power to be free of our suffering, and to help others be free of their suffering as well.

If you recognize the power you have to help others be free of their suffering, it is a gift, and not to use this gift is a waste of your power. Once you have realized that all things are one, the only thing to do is live your life in service to the all. True happiness comes from making others happy, and all of us have a creative way in which we can express ourselves and provide value to the lives of others.

To practice acting and behaving in a way that is supportive and not destructive of life is Right Action, and to practice Right Action is to practice mindful living—being deeply aware of life in this moment. To follow the Eightfold Path is not always easy, especially when we live in a society that is not supportive of such a pure, loving, and healing practice. Temptation to act in fear, to cause harm, and to live in illusion is everywhere in our society, but if the seeds of understanding, truth, and love, are strong within us, we will not lose our way.

If there are times when we do perform unwholesome acts, it is okay too. We should not be too hard on ourselves when we are walking this path, and should be able to relax and forgive ourselves when we act in an unwholesome way. However, we should also strive to live in a way that is harmonious with Truth, health, love, and life. Keeping the bigger picture in mind will help us stay true to the path and not lose ourselves in illusions and trivial matters. Right Action means most of all that our actions are rooted in love for all and not in gratification for ourselves alone.

Right Livelihood

Right Livelihood refers to the work that you do and the lifestyle you live, and whether or not that lifestyle is wholesome or unwholesome. To practice Right Livelihood, you must earn a living without going against your ideals of love and compassion. If our intention is to live for the good of all, we cannot work in a job that involves killing, stealing, sexual misconduct, lying, or selling drugs.

The way that you support yourself can be an expression of your deepest self, or it can be a source of suffering for yourself and others. If we work in an industry that produces toxic products and damages the well-being of others, we cannot practice Right Livelihood. Right Livelihood enables us to live in harmony with the Truth, with love, with kindness, and with awareness.

In our society, there are times when it is difficult to find a job. But if we work somewhere that causes harm to life, or pollutes the planet, we should try to find another job. The work that we do should be an expression of our true nature, not an expression of ignorance, violence, or ego.

Not only does working in a harmful industry create suffering for other living beings, but it infects our own consciousness, and contributes to our own suffering. If we work in an industry that pollutes the air, we are breathing in that air that we are polluting. Essentially, we are polluting ourselves.

To practice Right Livelihood requires that we practice mindfulness of our thoughts, words, and actions, and realize that our lives affect more than just ourselves, but impact the world as a whole. If we truly want to practice Right Livelihood, we should also be mindful of the way that we live our lives, and how our daily habits affect the health of our body.

This body is a blessing, and to mistreat the body will only limit your experience. By focusing on our diet and lifestyle, we dramatically improve the quantity and quality of our time spent on this earth. If our body is in good health, we will feel good, and we will not suffer from unnecessary illnesses. Food is the best medicine, and it is best used as a preventive medicine. We shouldn't wait until we are sick to focus on our health, but should focus on our health so we can feel great and won't have to worry about getting sick.

"When diet is wrong, medicine is of no use. When diet is correct, medicine is of no need."

– Ayurvedic proverb

Our body plays a major role in how we feel at each moment. When we are stressed or afraid, our body tenses up, our breathing becomes shallow, and our glands secrete cortisol into our bloodstream, which is severely harmful to our health. Many illnesses are caused simply because people are too stressed.

When we are happy and relaxed, hormones like dopamine, serotonin, and oxytocin are released into our bloodstream, which are good for our bodies and help us heal. By focusing on the health of our bodies, we improve the health of our minds. Or, as the Buddha said, *"To keep the body in good health is a duty... Otherwise we shall not be able to keep our mind strong and clear."*

By living a healthy lifestyle and doing what is best for our bodies, we also will be doing what is best for the planet. If we are focused on our health, we will not consume products that cause us harm, and will create a larger demand for companies that care about our health, and care about the health of our planet as well.

We might not realize it in our daily lives, but our diet impacts the whole of the earth. We have the power to create positive global change simply by consciously choosing to eat products that are good for our health, and avoiding products that hinder our health.

To practice Right Livelihood is to live our lives in a way that is supportive of life, and not harmful to life. And to practice Right Livelihood or any of the elements of the Eightfold Path, we must also be able to practice Right Diligence.

Right Diligence

Right Diligence, or Right Effort, refers to the intention with which we live our lives. It is the energy that helps us realize and consciously choose to live in alignment with the Eightfold Path. If we are diligent for possessions, sex, food, or fame, that is wrong diligence. To practice Right Diligence means to practice living in a way that does not cause suffering to oneself or others.

If we are meditating, doing yoga, or performing any kind of spiritual practice, but this practice is done with wrong intentions, or is done to take us further away from reality than deeper into it, we will not be practicing Right Diligence.

Intention is powerful. Everything that we do begins with an intention. How we decide to live our lives is based on the intentions that we have. We can become acutely aware of our intention and whether it is wholesome or unwholesome by practicing mindfulness of our thoughts, and what motivates us to do what we do.

Many ancient traditions realize the power that intention has in shaping our reality. Qigong masters proclaim that *"Qi (or chi) follows intent,"* which is similar to the more popular saying, *"energy flows where attention goes."* In the classic Vedic text of the Upanishads it states: *"You are what your deepest desire is. As your desire is, so is your intention. As your intention is, so is your will. As your will is, so is your deed. As your deed is, so is your destiny."*

Many people do not take the time to reflect on their mind and actions and ask themselves why it is that they do what they do. What is the motivating force in your life? Why do you live your life in the way that you do? Why do you think, speak, and act in the way that you do? What is your intention for life? Do you wish to improve the state of the world and benefit the lives of yourself and others? Or do you wish to only benefit yourself? Are you motivated by love or fear? Abundance or scarcity? What is your reason for living?

It is important to look into our motives and determine whether our intentions are pure or impure. By recognizing what the cause of our effort is, we can decide to give up doing the things that are not really in line with our desires, and can then give our energy and intention to things that are really important.

By becoming aware of the source of our efforts, we can have clarity on our path, and can hold our intentions firmly in our mind, thus giving us the energy we need to follow the path with understanding and awareness.

Right Mindfulness

Right Mindfulness is at the heart of the Eightfold Path. When we are mindful, our thinking is Right Thinking, our speech is Right Speech, our action is Right Action, and so on. Our attention is always focused on something, but often times our attention is not focused on our reality of the present moment, and causes us to be out of touch with reality by dwelling on our thoughts, fantasies, and mental illusions instead.

Right Mindfulness is to be conscious of the present moment, in the present moment. It is to have our attention here and now, and to give our heart, mind, and body, to our experience of the here and now. The Sanskrit word for mindfulness is *smriti*, which means "remember." Mindfulness is remembering to come back to the present moment whenever our attention is lost in our thoughts.

When our attention is focused on something that takes us away from the present moment, this is wrong mindfulness. When we dwell fully in the present moment, this is Right Mindfulness.

Right Mindfulness gives us insight and understanding, and without mindfulness, our actions might cause us to suffer, and might also cause others to suffer as well. Through mindfulness, we can be open to the present moment, and can have a deep understanding of what is an appropriate way to interact with life as it exist in this ever-changing moment.

Right Concentration

The practice of Right Concentration is to cultivate an awareness of the present moment—it is to cultivate a mind that is one-pointed. In China, some refer to concentration as "the abode of true mind." To live in this abode of true mind is to maintain equanimity, to maintain calmness, and to dwell on whatever happens in the present moment, even as it changes. A mind with Right Concentration does not try to grasp reality, but lets reality be reality.

"The perfect man employs his mind as a mirror; it grasps nothing; it refuses nothing; it receives, but does not keep."

– Chung-Tzu

It has been said that the highest wisdom is detachment. Many people have a misconception of what detachment is. Detachment is not that you should not care for anything, or should not own anything. Detachment means that you do not allow yourself to be upset by the course that nature takes. You understand the changing nature of reality, and do not cling to what no longer exists, as this only creates suffering.

To live in a state of detachment is to live in a state of freedom—freedom from all of the suffering caused by clinging to the phenomena of the ever-changing world. When one lives in a state of detachment, they do not have regrets for the past, or fears of the future. They let life take its course without attempting to interfere with its movement or change. They do not resist change or try to prolong the stay of something. Nor do they try to speed up the departure of something unpleasant. Instead, they move with life, and are in accord with the symphony of life as it plays its music. This is the nature of Presence, of Freedom, of Enlightenment.

This deep understanding of the ever-changing nature of reality enables us to remain focused on the present moment, regardless of how it changes form. This is Right Concentration. It is an active concentration which is different than the selective concentration we usually apply to the word concentration. To have Right Concentration is to remain centered in our awareness, to keep our attention on the present moment, and not to be lost in the grasping of our minds.

Selective concentration is also useful, such as when it comes to solving a difficult problem. But once we solve the problem, we do not cling to it in our minds, we let it go, and we continue to dwell on the present moment.

When we practice Right Concentration, our mind reflects reality as it is. We welcome whatever comes along, and we also allow it to pass freely. We do not think about or long for anything; we just dwell in the present moment with all of our being. When a bird flies over a lake, the lake holds the bird in its reflection. When the bird is gone, the lake lets the bird go, and reflects the clouds and the sky just as clearly. When the object of our concentration has passed, we do not struggle or try to hold onto it, we remain still, clear, and calm, just like the lake.

With Right Concentration, we embrace reality. We do not resist it or try to experience something other than what we are experiencing now. When we let go of this need to fix reality and force it to fit our desires, we are able to relax and be free from all of the unnecessary suffering that we inflict upon ourselves.

Right concentration leads to freedom, and freedom leads to happiness. To experience happiness, to experience peace, and to experience freedom, we must learn to live with our awareness in the present moment. All of the practices of the

Eightfold Path point one to a state of mindfulness, awareness, and Presence.

To live in this state is to be detached from both the past and future, and to live in the eternal dimension of here and now. Past and future are merely concepts—illusions—they have no existence apart from this moment. When we realize this deeply, and live in accord with this Truth, we are free from the need to be anywhere but here and now, and we realize that the here and now is the source of all joy, all happiness, and all freedom, as life is only ever happening now, and all that really exists is the reality that is happening in this very moment.

"You may believe yourself out of harmony with life and its eternal Now; but you cannot be, for you are life and exist Now—otherwise you would not be here. Hence the infinite Tao is something which you can neither escape by flight nor catch by pursuit; there is no coming toward it or going away from it; it is, and you are it. So become what you are."

— Alan Watts

---

23 Be YOU

In the "Lotus Sutra," a revered Buddhist text, the Buddha announces to thousands of beings that in teaching the Four Noble Truths, The Eightfold Path, the twelve interdependent arisings, and all of his other teachings, he had not taught them the full Truth. In hearing this, many of the beings attending his discussion felt wronged or unworthy, and decided to leave, but those that stayed demanded to know if they had not been taught the full Truth, then what was the actual Truth the Buddha had not taught?

After persistently asking the Buddha to share this Truth, he agreed. The Truth that the Buddha had not taught was that the Buddhahood of all sentient beings had already been achieved. There are no practices that can make you enlightened or can turn you into a Buddha, because you already are. This is the essence of Zen Buddhism—that there is nothing to do, nothing to accomplish, just to be and to live naturally in your own being is enough.

The premise of Zen is that all beings are in *Nirvana* from the beginning, and that all dualism is only falsely imagined. There is nothing we can do to get in accord with our true being as we are already it! In the words of the Cheng-tao Ke:

> *"Like the empty sky it has no boundaries,*
> *Yet it is right in this place, ever profound and clear.*
> *When you seek to know it, you cannot see it.*
> *You cannot take hold of it,*
> *But you cannot lose it.*
> *In not being able to get it, you get it.*
> *When you are silent, it speaks;*
> *When you speak, it is silent.*
> *The great gate is wide open to bestow alms,*
> *And no crowd is blocking the way."*

The true nature of the mind is, according to a Zenrin poem: *"like a sword that cuts, but cannot cut itself; like an eye that sees but cannot see itself."* The mind cannot grasp the mind, but through trusting our own nature, we can allow the mind to be. We can allow it to act spontaneously, and when we stop clinging to our mind we gain the freedom to behave naturally, to trust in the wisdom within us, and not to go against our own nature.

Much of our suffering arises from having a mind that is split against itself. But as Alan Watts said, *"If you cannot trust yourself, you cannot even trust your mistrust of yourself—so that without this underlying trust in the whole system of nature you are simply paralyzed."* We need to learn to stop clinging to our minds with our minds, and to allow our minds to just be. This form of surrender is necessary to attain freedom.

But we are afraid of surrender. The ego fears that it is going to lose everything, clinging to thought with all that it has. But there is nothing to lose except our illusions and the suffering they produce, and when we lose these there is no longer anything preventing us from being ourselves.

"Men are afraid to forget their own minds, fearing to fall through the void with nothing on to which they can cling. They do not know that the void is not really the void but the real realm of the Dharma... It cannot be looked for or sought, comprehended by wisdom or knowledge, explained by words, contacted materially (i.e., objectively) or reached by meritorious achievement."

— Huang-po

The whole spirit of Zen is to surrender our attachment to conceptual grasping, and to trust in our own nature, allowing ourselves to act spontaneously, without resistance. When we do this, our mind is free to express itself, free to act clearly in response to the moment, and free to behave without clinging, doubt, or mistrust in oneself.

We do not need to know how to use our glands, circulate our blood, or grow our hair. These things happen on their own—without our need to interfere. In the same way, we do not need to know how the mind functions in order to use it. Nor do we need to define life and know its meaning in order to live. All we need to do is Be.

Bruce Lee, a martial artist and follower of Zen philosophy, once said, *"In Buddhism there is no place for using effort. Just be ordinary and nothing special. Eat your food, move your bowels, pass water, and when you're tired go and lie down. The ignorant will laugh at me, but the wise will understand."* This is the type of natural living that is emphasized in Zen—to listen to your body, to act spontaneously, and to let your intuition guide you.

The Chinese word for Nature is *Ziran*, which means *"that which happens of itself."* Our lungs breathe by themselves, our nails grow by themselves, our eyes see by themselves—there is nothing we need to do to be in accord with nature, as we are nature; we just need to let nature be, and allow ourselves to be, so that we may live naturally and allow life to happen on its own. It is our clinging to life and our resistance to the way of nature that causes our suffering.

The Sanskrit word for intellect, *vikalpa*, means to divide and break apart. The intellect can only know reality by dividing it, but reality itself is not divided; it exists as one interconnected and unified entity. By definition, the intellect cannot understand the whole.

The word or concept "tree" is clearly not the same as an actual tree. When we experience a tree, we see the earth it grows in, the water and sunlight it absorbs, the insects crawling along its trunk, and this is all then interpreted individually by our feelings, memories, and associations. The tree is not a static, unchanging concept; it is a fluid always-changing experience. The intellect is not capable of understanding a tree in its totality, nor is it capable of understanding the totality of who we are, as we are just as much a fluid and changing experience as the tree.

Be YOU

In the classic Chinese tale of the snail and the centipede, a snail asks a centipede *"How do you move all those legs?"* When the centipede attempts to reply, he becomes utterly confused and is unable to move his legs at all.

We know very well who we are and how to live at the level of feeling and body-knowing, but when we are asked who we are, or how our body functions, and we attempt to define this experience with the intellect, we are unable to come up with a definition, and we become confused like the centipede in the Chinese tale. The reality of our being exists far beyond the intellect—beyond division, separation, or mental conceptualization.

The aim of Zen is to experience reality as it is, without the intellect interfering. This seems simple enough, but in our mind-dominant society, most are incapable of the simple act of observation without evaluation. We allow our thoughts to interfere with our experience, and rather than experiencing life, we experience a mental image of life—a perception filtered by thoughts, judgments, discriminations, and comparison.

Zen focuses on seeing life as it exists in each moment, feeling the moment deeply, and being aware of life as a whole, not as our mind fragments it with thought. Only in this state of pure awareness are we truly free to be.

"Zen master is not trying to give you ideas about life; he is trying to give you life itself, to make you realize life in and around you, to make you live it instead of being a mere spectator... A symphony is not explained by a mathematical analysis of its notes; the mystery of a woman's beauty is not revealed by a postmortem dissection; and no one ever understood the wonder of a bird on the wing by stuffing it and putting it in a glass case. To understand these things, you must live and move with them as they are alive. The same is true of the universe: no amount of intellectual analysis will explain it, for philosophy and science can only reveal its mechanism, never its meaning or, as the Chinese say, its Tao.

"What is the Tao?" A Zen master answers, "Usual life is the very Tao." "How does one bring oneself into accord with it?" "If you try to accord with it, you get away from it." For to imagine that there is a "you" that is separate from life which somehow has to accord with life is to fall straight into the trap... Self-consciousness is a stoppage because it is like interrupting a song after every note so as to listen to the echo, and then feeling irritated because of the loss of rhythm."

— Alan Watts

By trying to grasp at life, cling to it, and define it, we only separate ourselves from it. Of course this is only a conceptual separation, as you cannot really separate yourself from life, because you are life. But by dwelling in this mental realm of thinking, defining, judging, analyzing, evaluating, etc. we prevent ourselves from living comfortably, and prevent ourselves from flowing with life and realizing that we are a part of it.

Zen Buddhists realize that they are not separate from Nature, and they feel quite comfortable in Nature. They understand that Nature is everything, and you are a part of Nature. Therefore you are Nature, so allow yourself to be yourself and live naturally. Let go of the pressure of trying to become someone, of trying to escape yourself, or of trying to reach some level of success—you are already perfect as you are, you are already in *Nirvana*, you are already free—you only need to realize it.

By living in a society that is disconnected from Nature, we have become disconnected from our own nature. When you are in the forest, the desert, or the mountains, you see that everything is a part of the total environment, everything is a part of one unified whole. But in cities, we see blocks, buildings, streets, concrete, asphalt, metal, plastic, and things that make us appear separate from Nature.

By disconnecting from Nature physically, we have become disconnected from Nature spiritually as well. We can restore our connection to ourselves by restoring our connection to Nature, as the nature within us and the Nature outside of us are not two separate things.

It is not only Zen Buddhists that realize their oneness with Nature, but many other traditions as well. Native cultures are very in tune with their surroundings. Shamans recognize that everything is living and they are deeply aware of the connection they have to the natural world. They understand that we are all a part of one Spirit, and treat everything in regards to the Spirit that lives within them. They talk to the Universe, to the trees, and to the rocks, just as they would talk to human beings or animals. Everything has Spirit within it, and by seeing the Spirit that lies within every form we remember to treat everything with kindness, love, and respect.

"Everything that exists has Being, has God-essence, has some degree of consciousness.

Even a stone has rudimentary consciousness; otherwise, it would not be, and its atoms and molecules would disperse. Everything is alive. The sun, the earth, plants, animals, humans — all are expressions of consciousness in varying degrees, consciousness manifesting as form."

— Eckhart Tolle

If a single point of the Universe is conscious, then the whole Universe must be conscious. Native tribes and Eastern philosophers were able to recognize this fact, and the discovery of the holographic nature of the Universe shows that quantum physicists are beginning to recognize it, too. Everything is alive; everything has Spirit. But we cannot feel this Spirit and understand our connection to it by trying to grasp it, or define it with our minds. It is elusive, ungraspable, and unknowable, yet it is the essence of all things, and the essence of who we are as well.

To live in alignment with Spirit, we must learn to get out of our heads and into our hearts. We must learn to trust in our own nature. To do this might require that you meet yourself for the very first time. We have spent so much of our lives trying to escape ourselves, trying to define ourselves, or trying to become something other than ourselves. We have inflicted much suffering onto ourselves by doing this. To be free of this suffering, we have to calm our minds and tune in to our hearts.

By accepting ourselves as we are, we are finally able to be ourselves, and we become content with ourselves as we are in this moment. Once we reach this level of contentment and self-acceptance, we no longer compare ourselves to others, and we no longer fear what others will think of us. We drop all of our fears, and understand that what others perceive in us is a reflection of themselves, and we are not going to let their projections interfere with our happiness. To realize this fully is perhaps one of the most liberating feelings one can experience. When you no longer care what people think of you, you develop a level of freedom that no one can take away from you, the freedom to be yourself and to Love yourself unconditionally.

If your happiness is not dependent on the opinions of others, it won't matter to you what people think of you, because you will be happy regardless. Think of how much suffering is caused simply by comparing ourselves to others, by trying to be like others, or by worrying about what others will think of us. Can you see how all of this is just a reflection of our lack of self-acceptance? When you accept yourself fully, and love yourself as you are, all of these worries, fears, and insecurities just drop off, and you become absolutely free.

I like to think of this freedom as tuning into YOU. When you stop looking outward for answers, you look within, and tune into your heart. When you do this, you realize the answer to happiness, freedom, and love is not "out there," the answer is YOU; you have just been so out of touch with yourself that you have not experienced the freedom that comes from being yourself and allowing yourself to be who you naturally are.

A flower does not compete with the flower next to it; it just grows and blossoms in its own beauty. You, too, are a unique and beautiful expression of nature, and you too can flourish by growing and blossoming in the beauty of your own being. By trying to be something other than yourself, you take away the uniqueness that is YOU. No one can be you better than you can, and that is your power.

While we are all unique individuals, we are not separate from the whole of Nature. Just as the branches of a tree may be unique and different, but are not separate from the tree as a whole. You can embrace your individuality and uniqueness, while acknowledging and appreciating your connection to all living things.

Notice when you are suffering, when you are worrying about being judged, when you are living in fear, regret, anxiety, etc., and realize how these are taking you away from being in tune with YOU and the peace that comes from relaxing into your being in the present moment. Breaking free is not a violent act of destruction; it is a peaceful act in which you relax fully into the bliss of your own being.

When you accept YOU, and live in harmony with YOU, allowing yourself to be YOU, you realize the peace and freedom that comes from expressing yourself naturally without resistance, without fear, and without anything restricting you from living fully. To simply be content with yourself enables you to be content with all of life. By remaining centered in YOU, you don't mind what happens, as you are not dependent on anything or anyone for your peace, for you have found peace within the essence of your own being.

Jiddu Krishnamurti, was one of the greatest minds in history, and one of the best able to see through spiritual fantasies and cut through to the Truth of things. He did not believe in gurus, or spiritual teachers, but stated that *"Truth is a pathless land,"* and that if you are following someone else in search of Truth you will never find it.

Krishnamurti gave countless talks, in which he ironically implied that his audience shouldn't be listening to spiritual talks. In one of these lectures, Krishnamurti paused in the midst of his speech and said, *"Do you want to know what my secret is? I do not mind what happens."*

Instead of clinging to expectations, desires, wishes, or fantasies, Krishnamurti suggested that freedom comes from being content with whatever happens, and embracing the moment fully, without desiring for the moment to be different. He called this the "*freedom from the known*," freedom from the tyranny of the expected, and freedom from conceptual knowledge of what reality is, and how we have defined reality, and ourselves, according to this conceptual knowledge. He stated that, "*the highest form of intelligence is the ability to observe without evaluating,*" which is not unlike the Buddhist concept of mindfulness and Right Concentration.

The ability to be here now, without interfering with the mind, is the source of freedom and contentment. It is difficult for so many people to reach this state because they try to do so with their minds, but the mind cannot grasp it, and to be in this state one must learn to surrender the mind's need for intellectual understanding, and find comfort in the unknown.

"*We must not only cut asunder the snare of the mind and the senses, but flee also from the snare of the thinker, the snare of the theologian and the church-builder, the meshes of the Word and the Bondage of the Idea. All these are within us waiting to wall in the spirit with forms; but we must always go beyond, always renounce the lesser for the greater, the finite for the Infinite; we must be prepared to proceed from illumination to illumination, from experience to experience, from soul-state to soul-state... Nor must we attach ourselves even to the truths we hold most securely, for they are but forms*

*and expressions of the Ineffable who refuses to limit itself
to any form or expression."*

— Sri Aurobindo Ghose

Lao-Tzu, another one of history's great mystics, was well aware of the freedom and peace that comes from not grasping reality. One of his most famous sayings is, *"Life is a series of natural and spontaneous changes. Don't resist them—that only creates sorrow. Let reality be reality. Let things flow naturally forward in whatever way they like."*

Lao-Tzu wrote the "Tao Te Ching," a profound text full of wisdom, upon which the philosophy of Taoism was founded. But Lao-Tzu was not a Taoist, just as the Buddha was not a Buddhist, nor was Jesus a Christian. These people taught that the freedom we seek is within us, and that we will not find it through intellectual philosophy, religious dogma, or any form of outward seeking.

They taught that Truth is living, and we must learn to accept that it can't be confined to the limitations of words, or definitions, and that we must let life be life, we must let reality be reality, and we must let ourselves be ourselves.

Alan Watts once said, *"Waking up to who you are requires letting go of who you imagine yourself to be."* When we stop clinging to our definitions of Truth, we open ourselves up to what the Truth actually is. When we get out of our minds, out of the illusory realm of mental noise, out of the world of *maya*, we open ourselves up to the dimension of life—a dimension where time is only a concept, where all things are in a constant flow of movement, where words have no value, and where all things are possible. This realm is the realm where we find freedom, and as long as we cling to the familiarity of what is known, we will never know the Truth and beauty of the unknown.

No words, no books, no teachers, no concepts, beliefs or ideologies can ever confine the Truth of what is. To discover this Truth for yourself you must learn to tune into YOU and to trust in your own direct experience of life. No one else can give you a better understanding than the wisdom inherent within your own being.

You don't need a temple; your body is your temple. You don't need a teacher; life is your teacher. You don't need to look for the sacred; every moment is sacred. You don't need to look to your circumstances for peace; you need to find peace in your heart. You don't need to attain freedom; you are already free. If you feel imprisoned it is only because you do not realize your freedom, and are caught in the web of your thinking mind.

Surrender the need to grasp, the need to define, the need to know, and from this a deeper knowing will emerge—one that cannot be explained by words, but can only be understood through awareness. Trust in your own intuition and the guidance of Spirit. Let yourself be yourself and live naturally. Quiet the noise of the mind, so that the wisdom of your heart may speak.

Be YOU

No amount of searching outward will ever bring you to the level of freedom that comes from searching within. The answer to ending your suffering, the answer to finding peace, to finding love, to finding freedom, is within you always. The answer is YOU. So allow yourself to be YOU, and to embrace the uncertainties of life. Just by finding peace within the essence of your own being you will find freedom from the chaos in the world. And as physicist David Bohm said, *"It is not possible for disorder to exist in a Universe that is ultimately unbroken and whole."*

While you may have an individual experience, you are indeed a part of the whole, and by being your natural self, you allow the whole to express itself freely through you. Trust in the wisdom of your own being, and enjoy the experience of life in whatever way it presents itself. Everything is a part of the greater whole that is YOU, and by surrendering your idea of separation, you experience the state of wholeness where nothing is divided, and where all things are one. It is in this state of undivided wholeness where you will experience freedom, where you will find joy, and where you will live life to the fullest, simply by allowing yourself to be YOU.

The Answer Is YOU

"There are no appearances at all apart from those that
originate in the mind.
The unimpeded nature of mind assumes all manner of
appearances.
Yet, though these appearances arise, they are without
duality.
And they naturally subside into the modality of mind,
Like waves in the water of an ocean.
Whatever names are given to these unceasingly arising
objects of designation,
In actuality, there is but one single nature of mind,
And that single nature of mind is without foundation and
without root.
Therefore, it is not perceptible at all, in any direction
whatsoever.
It is not perceptible as substance, for it lacks inherent
existence in all respects.
It is not perceptible as emptiness, for it is the resonance of
awareness and radiance.
It is not perceptible as diversity, for it is the indivisibility
of radiance and emptiness.
This present intrinsic awareness is manifestly radiant and
clear.
And even though there exists no known means by which
it can be fabricated,
And even though this awareness is without inherent
existence,
It can be directly experienced.
Thus, if experientially cultivated, all beings will be
liberated."

– The Tibetan Book of the Dead

The Answer Is YOU

About the Author

Joseph P. Kauffman is the founder of Conscious Collective, LLC—a societally oriented firm dedicated to awakening humanity from ignorance and participating in the evolution of human consciousness. Joseph also holds a certification in Permaculture Design from the Paititi Institute at Larapata Hatunpata, Peru. Driven by the philosophy of the Bodhisattva, he is passionate about helping others find peace and healing the suffering that exists on this planet.

conscious-collective.com

Instagram: @conscious_collective

Facebook: facebook.com/consciouscollective1111

The Answer Is YOU

Other Books by Joseph P. Kauffman:

"Conscious Collective: An Aim for Awareness"

"Stillness: A Guide to Finding Your Inner Peace"

"Oneness: Awakening From the Illusion of Separation"

"Just Be: A Small Book with a Big Message"

44335225R00143

Made in the USA
Middletown, DE
03 June 2017